Two Medics, One Nurse and a Gob Doctor

(Two wars in Iraq without fighting)

By

Brian (Harry) Clacy

This book is dedicated to all soldiers serving in the:

Royal Army Medical Corps, Queen Alexandra's Royal Army Nursing Corps, Royal Army Dental Corps and the Royal Logistic Corps.

Without their courage, skill, dedication, and professionalism, the entire British Army would be in a whole world of shit and pain.

Acknowledgments:

Two years ago I called in to see my friend Mick Killeen at his house in Beverley, he only lives about 10 minutes walk from my house. I had an idea about a book I had always wanted to read, but no-one had written it yet, I wanted to write about what soldiers serving in the Army Medical Services of the British Army see and do in a war environment, not the blood and guts, just the ordinary day to day stuff. I wanted to write a book about the things he had seen and done whilst serving out in Iraq, in his strong Yorkshire accent he bluntly told me, "Bloody hell mate, if you want to write a book about my war experiences it will be the smallest and most boring book ever written!" With a certain amount of bewilderment he agreed to take part in the book and I have spent many hours at his house drinking tea and listening to stories about his life and experiences in the second Iraq war. Far from being bored, I have laughed until my sides ached and have been amazed at the things he has told me.

The same applies to the other participants in the book, Sharon Anthony, Ritchie John and of course my own son Matt Fairclough, I am truly amazed at your patience with me; and your indifference at what you have all been through. I have never been to war and had to experience the uncertainty, discomfort and emotions you all went through. I just hope you feel I have done justice in my writing to all we have talked about.

I know this is an anomalous thing for a married man to do, but I have to give a big thank you to my Mother-in-law Joyce Chapman, her knowledge of the English language is astounding.... for a Yorkshire woman. I'm sorry Joyce, but it really should be pronounced Whitefriargate and not Whitefrageat. My apologies to the good people of Hull.

I like to give a big thank you to Miss Tracy Carter from Kirton Lindsey who has been a big help in proof reading my work and who has also encouraged me in my writing. I would also like to give her a belated thank you for all her help on the punctuation in my first book 'Harry was a Crap Hat'.

The following people have all helped, advised, encouraged and generally annoyed me at various stages of writing this book, from the Defence School of Transport, Major (Retired) Terry Cavender RCT, Staff Sergeant Eddie Ward RLC and Mrs Irene Renwick, my sister Susan, Major 'Smurf' Foulger of HQ 2 Medial Brigade and of course my ever helpful literary and medical guru Adam Broom (Paramedic) from Milton Keynes. Without the assistance you all gave me, I could have finished this book six months earlier.

I would also like to mention Eric Hartley of ELK Marketing and Planning Ltd who are based in Beverley East Yorkshire, Eric designed and produced the book cover for Two Medics, One Nurse and a Gob Doctor.

Last, but by no means least, a big thank you to the woman who has given me everything, including a polite and gentle kick up the arse when I needed it, my beautiful wife Nicky.

<u>Preface</u>

This isn't a book about super heroes who have gone through a torturous selection process to join the Paras, Royal Marines, or SAS. If you want to read that sort of story then go a little bit further along the bookshelf and pick up any one of the many books written by Ex Special Forces soldiers who have saved the world, all around the world.

This is a simple story about three ordinary men and a woman who served within the Army Medical Services during the first and second Gulf Wars, four soldier's who don't believe they are heroes, they merely joined the British Army and unfortunately ended up going to war. Only one of them was Regular Army and the other three were serving in the Territorial Army when they were called up. None of them particularly wanted to go to war but they had been trained to do a job within the British Army organization and they did exactly that. Mind you, the Regular Army soldier didn't exactly go without whinging and whining, but as anyone who has served within the Armed Forces knows, if you don't complain, you obviously don't understand the situation.

This book also doesn't contain details of Blood, Guts, and Glory; all that sort of bullshit is reserved for 'Commando' and 'Battle' comic books. I have written about what it is like for the Army Medical Services to live day to day in a modern desert war environment and some of the things they saw and felt. Some are funny, some bizarre, and others are very sad. I have also given an insight to how the RAMC (Royal Army Medical Corps) and RADC (Royal Army Dental Corps) carry out their war roles, and the way soldiers on the ground sometimes ignore army directives and conduct things in a more sensible manner.

This book contains a small profile on each of the soldiers concerned which is followed by their individual intersected 'war stories' that includes some mundane but interesting facts, and finally the book contains an epilogue on each of them, how they felt after the war and what they are doing now.

As I have already stated, this isn't a book about macho super heroes who have bayoneted and bludgeoned our Government's enemies into submission, after all it's easy to kill a man, teenagers, and drunken morons are doing exactly that on the streets of Britain most Saturday nights. But what's involved in helping the sick and wounded after they have been injured in a war and who are the soldiers who have to carry out these mainly unsung duties?

Well, these are four such soldiers, and what they experienced.

Harry Clacy

PROFILES

Corporal Mick Killeen
Royal Army Medical Corps
(Territorial Army)
Combat Medical Technician Class 2

Second Gulf War – 26 February 2003 to 17 July 2003

Mick Killeen was born in 1954 and describes himself as a working class Yorkshire man, he stands 6 ft 3 ins in his socks and weighs about 14 ½ stone, so you can hardly call him rotund. The word beanpole springs to mind. As you look up at his short thick grey hair he is strikingly reminiscent of what Stan Laurel probably looked like in his mid fifties. He has a typical Yorkshire wit that is drier than a James Bond Martini.

Born in Doncaster he has spent the majority of his life in and around Beverley in East Yorkshire. His mother Muriel Killeen worked as a civil servant in the local Labour Exchange and his dad Les deserted her when Mick was just six weeks old. Les left Muriel with four older sons and an eldest daughter; he married another woman with whom he had another two children. Mick knows very little about his dad and is indifferent about the subject. What he does know is Les Killeen was a Hull man who served in the Royal Green Jackets as a Territorial Soldier during the early part of World War Two. He was mobilised for war from Wenlock Barracks in Hull (the same place Mick would be mobilised for war almost sixty years later) and was wounded in the ankle during the evacuation of the British Army from Dunkirk. When released from hospital he served as a motorcycle dispatch rider in the UK for the rest of the war, he was medically downgraded as a result of the injury and was probably deemed unfit to continue soldiering in the Infantry.

8

Muriel divorced Les in 1954 and with no father about Mick grew up idolising his brother Graham who was a very good looking 'Jack the Lad'. Mick followed his brother everywhere and firmly believed his brother had an interest in Flora and Fauna, as he seemed to enjoy walks on Beverley Westwood with all of his girlfriends. Younger brothers can be a pain in the neck to their older siblings because they are oblivious to the need for privacy in the art of seduction.

At school all four brothers were nicknamed 'Killer' for which Mick has no explanation; he thinks it was more than likely because it simply rhymes with Killeen. During his time in the Territorial Army Mick always introduced himself as 'Killer', and is still known as that today. Mick attended Woodmansey Primary before moving up to Longcroft School where he was an average but attentive student, however, he left school without any academic qualifications.

At the age of fourteen Mick felt his time would be put to better use bringing in some money for the family rather than wasting time on further education, so he went to work as a labourer for a market gardening firm. In 1969 he had an accident with a broken pane of glass from one of the greenhouses, it sliced off two of his fingers that were successfully sewn back on to his hand but he ended up 'on the sick' for about nine months. When his hand was fully healed Mick went to work for an Engineering Firm in Beverley called Deans but was only employed as a labourer and spent most of his time sweeping the floors. A vacancy opened one day for an engineering apprentice and Mick was persuaded to "Go for it," he was up against young men who had 'A' Levels and didn't think he had a realistic chance of getting the job. Mick believes his life has been governed by destiny and nothing has been planned. There may be some truth in that because his peers and superiors had declared him 'a good lad' and that was enough to secure him the placement.

The job involved working on lathes, drills and grinding machines as well as a considerable amount of welding, Mick enjoyed the work and the company of his Colleagues. He met and worked with an 18-year-old lad called Andy who became his best friend, the pair of them took all the skills they learned at Deans and started making their own personal firearms. They put their very inquisitive and ingenious heads together to produce a machine gun that fired .22 calibre ammunition, and cross bows that could kill an elephant and a 12 bore shotgun pistol that would have broken Geoff Capes' wrists. If that wasn't frightening enough, they set about making their first and only bomb. They used a metal container for the body of the bomb and a mixture of carbide and a chemical used for degassing aluminium for the explosive. To ignite the bomb they made a fuse using a magnesium tablet wrapped in cloth and inserted it into the middle of the bomb before sealing the completed Improvised Explosive Device. The location for testing the bomb was dictated by the need for water and the ability to keep them at a safe distance from ground zero when it exploded. The lads knew that Magnesium erupts when exposed to water and that would hopefully ignite the homemade explosive in the bomb. Mick and Andy "Hoyed the bomb off Weel Bridge" during their lunch break to see if it worked, Weel Bridge was not far along the canal from Deans and Beverley shipbuilding yard. They could see the device bubbling away on the bottom of the canal but that seemed to be the only resulting action of their rather pathetic bomb, so they started to walk back to work along the canal. As they approached Deans Engineering an ear splitting explosion sent a thirty-foot plume of water up into the air, the bomb had worked and this resulted in hundreds of workers from Beverley shipyard evacuating their workplace because they believed Deans Engineering had suffered a gas explosion. Mick and Andy decided to retire from the Armaments industry.

Andy was a Territorial soldier and used to talk to Mick about his weekends of shooting, cross country driving and the drinking of copious amounts of beer. He was an RCT (Royal Corps of Transport) Driver with 250 Field Ambulance at Wenlock Barracks in Hull and persuaded Mick to come along to a Drill Night one Thursday evening. Mick was intrigued, he spent most of his weekends lazing about at home, and from the way Andy described things, enlisting into the TA would be great fun. The Recruiting Team at 250 Field Ambulance tried to coerce Mick into joining the unit as a Medic because that was the vacant trade they needed filling more than any other. Mick was having none of that, he wanted to drive a Bedford R L three tonner like his mate Andy and if he couldn't do that he was leaving straight away. The unit relented and Mick became Potential Driver Killeen.

He attended a Basic Training Course at the Territorial Army Training Camp in Grantham Lincolnshire and Passed Out as the Best Recruit of the course. If you speak to any soldier in the British Army, other than those in the Household Division, they will all tell you how much they hate doing Drill, marching up and down a Drill Square all day long is about the biggest pain in the arse you can get in soldiering. Perversely, Mick revelled in Drill and all the bullshit that goes hand in hand with it, pressing his uniform, and bulling his boots were a pleasure not purgatory. Years later after Mick and his girlfriend Jean married they had two daughters, Rachel and Victoria, much to their bemusement he used to bull their school shoes every night. To avoid being ridiculed by their friends they would deliberately scuff their shoes down the garden path before anyone saw them.

Before deploying on Exercise Crusader in 1980, 250 Field Ambulance had to address the problem of not having sufficient Radio Operators within the unit. Captain Sandy Darling was the Motor Transport Officer who had to resolve the problem; he had to find the soldiers from his RCT Drivers to fill the shortfall. He assembled all members of the RCT detachment on Parade to explain his problem and asked for volunteers to go on a Radio Operators Course. In the army you learn from an early stage that you do not volunteer for anything, and true to this ethos not a man on Parade moved for fear of it being taken as a sign of willingness to go on the dreaded Course. Captain Sandy Darling sighed and got over the negative response by saying "Right, OK then, you, you and you are the three volunteers!" Mick was one of the 'you's.'

He went on the Course and found it challenging but surprisingly enjoyable, working on the old style C 42 radios and using Morse Code seemed to be the job specially made just for him. He had the confidence and natural ability to work on a radio network with out getting flustered, even with lots of panicking officers around him. Mick also points out that Radio Operators are always dry, well fed and kept supplied with brews whilst on Exercise, it seemed a win, win situation.

It was a role that Mick played and became synonymous with in 250 Field Ambulance for the next 20 years until he reached his 45th birthday. In the Territorial Army you are deemed to be too old at that age to be an RCT soldier, you are then asked to leave or retrain in another trade. Mick

12

hated the thought of being a medic, which was the new trade he was offered, but he loved the Territorial Army so much that he would bear it just so that he could stay in the unit with all his mates. He would rather have been a chef but the Training Officer surreptitiously didn't give Mick all of his possible options for retraining. Before leaving school Mick had briefly wanted to train as a chef when his brothers worked in the Beverley Arms Hotel.

All Combat Medical Technician Courses are held at Keogh Barracks in Ash Vale near Aldershot, Mick attended and passed the Course with his usual diligence and resigned himself to working in 250 Field Ambulance Dressing Station or in one of the Medical Sections when he returned to the unit. He didn't consider the fact that the Territorial Army tick all the necessary boxes but can then work a nice flanking manoeuvre. He was too good a Radio Operator and too crap a medic not to be employed in his best skill. The unit let him carry on in his usual role whilst wearing an RAMC cap badge. Mick continued attending weekend exercises and Drill Nights without a thought of ever having to use any of his military skills for real, let's face it, he and the rest of NATO had been waiting over fifty years for the men in furry hats to come out from behind that dreaded Iron Curtain. The Berlin wall had now been taken down and apart from a bit of sabre rattling in the Middle East there wasn't any realistic chance of him ever going to war. He was Territorial Army and they would be a last resort if anything happened, and anyway a political solution would be found before he was called out of Wenlock Barracks in Hull. Unfortunately for Mick, lightning was about to strike twice in the same spot for the Killeen family.

Captain Sharon Anthony
QARANC
(Territorial Army)
Nurse

Second Gulf War – 14 March 2003 to 21 May 2003

Sharon Lesley Anthony had always wanted to be a nurse; as far back as she can remember there was nothing else she wanted to do. Born on 20th December 1961 in the house her parents still live in, she has grown up and lived in and around Hull all her life. Yet when you talk to her she lacks that harsh Hull accent, if she bought a scarf that cost one penny under £10, she wouldn't tell you it cost "Narn Narnty Narn." Sharon is a quietly spoken, articulate, friendly, and well educated woman who outwardly appears extremely confident, she describes herself as a sensible optimist who always sees the good in people. The thought of serving in the British Army was the furthest thing from her mind whilst growing up; her dad didn't have the choice though in the early 1950's.

Sharon's dad Harry Driffill was called up to do his National Service after the Korean War had started; he joined the Royal Engineers and was rapidly promoted to the rank of Corporal. He volunteered for an overseas deployment and was looking forward to a tour of duty in West Germany after his two-week embarkation leave; he was then given some good and bad news. The good news was he could go back home on leave for another two weeks; the bad news was he wasn't going to West Germany for his overseas deployment; he was going to the harsh and bloody environment of the Korean War.

14

On completion of his tour in South East Asia he came home and left the army and worked in the public health sector, in today's world he would be called an Environmental Health Inspector. On his demob the War Department gave him several options to complete his army reserve commitment, the one he took was to do 3 ½ years in the TA (Territorial Army) who were only expected to do Home Defence in the event of National Emergencies. He was not allowed to keep the rank he had reached during his National service and joined a Royal Engineer TA unit in Hull as Sapper Harry Driffill; he worked his way up to the rank of Staff Sergeant before being commissioned in the same unit as a Captain. Sharon remembers as a child going into the Officers' Mess to help her dad put up decorations for the Summer and Christmas Balls. In the 1960's after 12 years service he left the TA because the Government of the day started cutting back on expenditure and a lot of TA units were being merged together. His unit has long since been disbanded but the iron bridges he and his RE comrades built over some dykes in Bransholme are still there today, Sharon called them 'Daddy's Bridges' when she was a child. Harry and his wife Jackie had three children and Sharon was the middle one, she had an older brother and younger sister.

Sharon did well at senior school even though she was the only 'Non Catholic' pupil at the all girls Roman Catholic School in Hull, religion was a key factor in the school environment and the teachers tried to enlighten Sharon but she wouldn't have any of it. She must have been a good student in everything else though because she graduated with seven O Levels, included in these passes were Human Biology and Chemistry, which were obligatory for a career in medicine. Sharon wasn't exactly a goodie two shoes though because twice she 'twagged' off school, the first time after spending the day at home she darted out the back door as her big brother came home from his school, Sharon then ran round to the front of the house and nonchalantly walked in behind him two minutes later trying to look as if she'd had a hard day at school. On the second occasion Sharon heard her brother come into the house as he did a bit of 'twagging' himself. Fearful of getting into trouble with her big brother and getting 'spragged' on, she hid under her parents' bed for three hours until her brother went out again. 'Twagging' wasn't worth all the hassle that went with it so Sharon never did it again.

At the age of eleven Sharon joined the St Johns Ambulance Brigade and took part in Local and Regional first aid competitions and her local unit twice qualified for the National Finals. In the competitions there were team, individual and home nursing exams, the teams were also evaluated as they treated casualties with simulated wounds in a car crash scenario. She was never fazed by the blood and gore and learned to deal with everything in a calm and logical order, it was a good grounding for her future career in the world of nursing.

After leaving school, Sharon enrolled as a student on an 18-month pre-nursing course at Hull College; she did day release placements at HRI (Hull Royal Infirmary) children's ward and Delapole Psychiatric Hospital. Working on the children's ward confirmed Sharon's wish to work with children when she eventually graduated. At Delapole, Sharon spent most of her time arranging flowers and chasing after elderly ladies with senile dementia, for this she was paid the princely sum of £90 a month. In 1976 this was quite a good income for a 17 year old pre-student nurse and like all good student nurses, past, present and probably future, the majority of it was spent on alcohol and partying. Sharon made friends with a fellow student nurse who was a big rugby fan of Hull FC and she accompanied her to the home and away matches. In 1978 Sharon and her friend joined a coach party to watch Hull FC play an away game against Blackpool; they were the only two females on the coach. It was an overnight trip and the two girls shared a room at a Bed and Breakfast accommodation in Preston, the men were lodged in a separate hotel just up the road. Sharon's mate 'copped off' with one of the lads on the coach and took him back to the B & B for some horizontal aerobic training, Sharon was left in a bit of a quandary, she could hardly lie in bed pretending to be asleep listening to the rampant love makers in the next bed. So she went back to the men's B & B and played cards until the early hours of the morning with a bloke called Mick Anthony and the other lads, when their lucky mate came back with a big cheesy grin on his face Sharon finally returned to her own B & B and got some sleep.

A few days after the Blackpool trip Sharon got a phone call from Mick asking her if she fancied going out for a drink, she couldn't recall exactly which of the lads he was but thought 'What the hell, it's a night out'. She recognised Mick straight away when they met in the pub and he told her that he'd actually got her phone number from a mutual rugby fan friend. You could tell Mick was a prop forward for his local rugby team by his build; he was and still is a stocky, confident, and typical northern bloke who has a smile not unlike a Cheshire Cat. The two of them became an item and after just one year of her Student Nurse placement at a Liverpool Hospital (She chose Liverpool for her placement so she could get to see Liverpool FC, and the legs of Kenny Dalglish and Kevin Keegan) she decided to quit so she could marry Mick and start a family.

They lived with Mick's mum and dad until they could afford to buy their own two up, two down house on Holderness Road where Sharon raised their two children Stephen and Donna. By 1981 Mick was working for the BP refinery in Hull and was still playing rugby, as a result of the latter he picked up a lot of injuries. He had a black eye when they got married, had a dislocated shoulder when Stephen was born and suffered from a ripped tendon in his finger on their first wedding anniversary. When they celebrated with a romantic meal in a restaurant Mick ate his food with a fork wedged into the huge padding that engulfed his hand. In 1986 a work Colleague at BP told Mick about his adventures as a member of 250 Field Ambulance RAMC which was one of several TA units in Hull, Mick's rugby injuries were literally becoming a pain, and the TA sounded like a challenge that might be good fun, he gave up rugby and started part time soldiering instead. By 2001 Mike was a Combat Medical Technician Class 1 and had worked his way up to the rank of Sergeant. At the same time Saddam Hussein had sent his forces to invade Kuwait, the British Regular and Territorial Army's were mobilised to remove them. Mick was determined to get involved but BP said they could not guarantee his job would be kept open for him if he volunteered, if the MOD called him up, that would be a different matter and they would re-employ him on his return. Much to Mick's chagrin he was never called up.

After Stephen and Donna reached school age Sharon decided to continue with her training to finally become a qualified nurse. She started as a student nurse in HRI on the Monday after the Hillsborough disaster involving the fans of Liverpool FC. She was now a mother and this fact alone confirmed her wish now, not to work with children. When she graduated three years later, of the twenty nurses who had graduated only six of them got a job in nursing, the jobs available were few and far between. For two years Sharon worked on the Gynaecological Ward at Princess Royal Hospital that she describes as, "All hormones and tears." She then spent six years on the Medical Wards at HRI, which later changed to a Medical Admissions Unit with only twenty-eight beds available for admissions. "It was a very busy and exciting place to work" says Sharon, "It really was a buzz, you never knew what was coming through the doors, and it could be anything from someone suffering a heart attack to a casualty with internal bleeding. We also had a high dependency unit where we had to do barrier nursing because of the problems of cross infections." Even though Sharon absolutely loved the job, by the year 2000 she was burnt out with the stress so she changed jobs and started working with a Government run charity, she helped drug addicts in Goole and Hull kick their addictions. This involved assessing addicts and putting a package of care and treatment together for them, she later changed jobs again and did virtually the same job but working with Her Majesty's Prison Service. Sharon visited and worked in some of the toughest and most dangerous prisons in Yorkshire, these included Leeds, Hull, and Lincoln, she also worked in Wakefield's women's prison. When she was wolf whistled in one of the prisons Sharon casually shouted, "You need some new glasses mate!"

By the time her children had reached the age of sixteen and fourteen Sharon decided to try and enlist in the TA herself, she had enjoyed the social side of Mick's TA life in the Corporal's and Sergeant's Mess at 250 Field Ambulance, but was reticent to step on his toes at the Hull unit. Sharon applied to join 212 Field Hospital at Sheffield but was turned down when on the medical she mentioned that on a few occasions she had suffered from migraines. Mick persuaded Sharon to fill an application form to join 250

Field Ambulance, as he wouldn't be concerned if she was in the same unit as him. Unfortunately she was turned down for the vacancy as a female officer because if she were commissioned she wouldn't be able to mix with the likes of her husband who was only a Sergeant?

When 250 Field Ambulance applied to take part in the 1996 Nijmegen Marches in Holland they didn't have enough volunteers to make up a full team. The prospect of marching 25 miles a day for four days seemed to put a lot of soldiers in the unit off, Sharon was drafted in to make up the numbers as a 'pretend' officer cadet, she agreed to help them out as long as they would consider offering her a place within the unit as a Nursing Officer. They were over a barrel and that's how Sharon became Lieutenant Sharon Anthony QARANC, but not before an interview at Brigade Headquarters and attending a two week Junior Officers Course at the RAMC Depot in Keogh Barracks near Aldershot. Before going on the Course Sharon pounded the pavements around Hull to improve her fitness, Mick told her she would fail the entire Course if she didn't pass a BFT (Basic Fitness Test) that is a three-mile run. He told Sharon that at her age the run must be completed in less than 27 minutes. The day before she went to Aldershot Sharon had got her BFT time down to 30 minutes and thought that as the BFT was in the second week of the Course, she would lose the extra three minutes as she went through the training and continued to improve on her fitness. On the actual BFT Sharon pushed herself to run as fast as she could but still failed to break the 27-minute benchmark, as she came in the PTI shouted out the time, "Lieutenant Anthony…28 minutes 17 seconds." Sharon shouted, "Oh sod it….I'll go and pack my bags now, I can't possibly run the BFT in under 27 minutes, I know I've failed!" The confused PTI looked at her and said, "What are you talking about Ma'm, females of

your age are allowed 30 minutes to complete the BFT."
Mick's little white lie had motivated Sharon to push herself
harder than she needed too, but at least she had passed and
was now a Lieutenant in the Queen Alexandra's Royal
Army Nursing Corps.

The Commanding Officer at 250 Field Ambulance asked
Sharon to teach First Aid to the latest recruits within the
unit, her time in the St Johns Ambulance was now going to
pay dividends.   Over the next few years 250 Field
Ambulance expanded, a new Section was formed in
Castleford and the detachment required a Section Officer.
By now Sharon had been promoted to Captain and she was
appointed to the position. After taking over she supervised
their training and checked all the Sections equipment, both
medical and military. It was her job to make sure everyone
in her Section was properly trained and ready if called up to
go to war. That's exactly what did happen, a total of fifty
officers and soldiers, both male and female, who included
some of Sharon's Section, received their call up papers to go
out to Iraq. Some of them turned to Sharon for reassurance
and advice about the prospect of their first operational
deployment. She felt guilty and envious that some of her
Section was deploying, just as Mick had agonised back in
2001, she began to think, 'I wonder why the MOD haven't
sent my call up papers?' She wouldn't be wondering for
much longer.

Lance Corporal Matt Fairclough
Royal Army Medical Corps
(Territorial Army)
Combat Medical Technician Class 2

Second Gulf War – 26 February 2003 to 21 July 2003

Matt's biological father deserted him, his mum and 18-month-old sister Naomi when he was just five years old. He was born in Kings Lynn Norfolk on the 1st of July 1970 but both his parents were raised in London. His father Tony Fairclough originally came from Croydon in South London, and his mum Ronnie (Veronica), although born in Chelmsford Essex just after the war in 1947, was raised in the Borough of Forest Gate in the East End of London. After the war a lot of the London midwifery was done in the Home Counties because of the poor condition of the Capital's hospitals, a lot of the damage done by the Luftwaffe during the Blitz had yet to be repaired.

Matt never knew his Grandfather on his mums' side of the family because he died before Matt was born but Dennis Bloomfield was a real East Ender, a proper cockney. Dennis enlisted into the Royal Artillery at the outbreak of World War Two and served in the Desert Campaigns in the Middle East. After the war Dennis returned home to his wife Gwen and eventually ran a newsagents shop in Forrest Gate, he also trained the local boys in a nearby boxing club. He was a large and tough but witty man who was held in high esteem in the Forrest Gate community. During the war Gwen was pestered by her milkman with double entendre and smutty remarks about how he could stand in for Dennis while he was away, he had taken a shine to her because she was a young, very slim and attractive woman. One day in 1946 the milkman opened Gwen's back door to deliver her pint of milk and shouted "Hello dahlin, it's only me, the man of your dreams." A recently demobbed Dennis came through to the kitchen wearing Gwen's house coat that was stretched to bursting point by his burley torso and growled, "Oooh lavley, cam in sweet'art and make all my dreams come true!" Gwen's bottle of milk smashed on the kitchen floor as the milkman ran for his life. Thereafter the Gold Top was delivered in silence and with a great deal of reverence.

Matt's father, Tony, was a tall slightly built and very good looking man who could charm the knickers off a woman at 300 meters. Several years after their marriage Tony and his mum Ronnie moved to Fordham in Essex after he started working for Lloyds of London. In the 1960's and early 1970's a lot of people commuted to work every day from Essex to London. Tony became involved in the drug scene of the time and was a regular at the Windmill Club where he often scored with both women and drugs. One particular night at the club Tony had the shit kicked out of him by a disgruntled soldier from Colchester Garrison; soldiers don't like it when puffy haired civvies try to pick up their wives and girlfriends. According to Tony the whole incident was a misunderstanding and the fight involved five soldiers against him, months later he told Ronnie that he eventually hunted down all the soldiers and pistol-whipped them to within an inch of their lives. Credence to this story is open to conjecture, as Tony only had a very brief and unsuccessful career when he joined the Territorial Army, he could talk the talk but couldn't walk the walk. Ronnie became exasperated with his affairs and they both moved about twelve miles to a semi-detached house in Sible Hedingham to make a new start. Tony made a new start all right, a new start on his married neighbour Janet who was a leggy blonde. Tony and Janet at least had the decency to wait until Matt's sister

Naomi was born before running away to start a new life together in South London. Ronnie was eventually evicted from the house in Sible Hedingham as she had no job and couldn't pay the mortgage. Braintree Council housed the three of them in a three-bed roomed, post war prefabricated home; it was in the roughest part of town and home to some of the roughest people.

After Ronnie divorced Tony she started dating, and eventually married, a young RCT (Royal Corps of Transport) soldier called Harry Clacy; it was around this time that Matt believes he had an epiphany. He moved to West Germany with Ronnie, Naomi and his new dad Harry and became mesmerized by anyone and anything that was military; at a young age he started reading books on a multitude of military matters. He adapted to living in a different country and was excited when armed soldiers started patrolling the Oerlinghausen Married Quarter estate and his local school; this was to protect Service families from any possible threat of violence during the terrorist Bader Meinhoff Group Campaign in the 1970's. Tony came out to Germany to visit Matt and Naomi and stayed with them at Harry and Ronnie's Army Married Quarter during his weeklong visit. Arrangements were made for a friend to pick Tony up from Hanover Airport because Harry was on a Guard Duty at Catterick Barracks in Bielefeld when Tony arrived. The duty finished at 0900 hours on Saturday morning and the Duty Driver took Harry home in a Land Rover, as Matt stood on the balcony of the flat he heard the Army Land Rover approaching and watched as Harry got out after it stopped. He shouted "Dads home" to anyone who was listening and ran down the stairs to meet him. Tony was not amused or impressed and unfortunately for Matt and Naomi that was the last they have seen of him up to date.

At school Matt was a scholastic nightmare, he was always acutely aware of being the new boy as he started at yet another SCS (Services Children's School), it is one of the tribulations for Servicemen's children when their fathers are posted from one Garrison to another. That could not be used as an excuse for Matt's poor schoolwork though, basically, the only thing that interested him in any of the academic syllabus was a study of the Nazi persecution of the Jews in World War Two. He was generally a lazy little sod. Matt and Naomi were presented with a baby brother, Daniel, who was born in June 1978 and although Naomi was initially quite jealous of him it was unfounded, Harry loved them all equally. Matt moved from school to school every time Harry was posted to a new unit. On one particular posting to Wolfenbuttel Garrison on the East/West German border, Matt was told he, like all the other Service children in Wolfenbuttel Garrison who were over 11 years old, would have to attend a Service Boarding school in Rheindahlen. The Boarding School in Rheindahlen was located on the Dutch/German Border and involved an eight-hour drive by coach to get there. Ronnie hated him being so far away, but the school dormitory was a familiarisation of barrack room life that would prepare Matt for his own service career.

Matt eventually left school when Harry was posted to SEME (School of Electrical and Mechanical Engineering) in Borden Hampshire. He worked in a civil engineering firm called Action Hose Couplings, a local butchers shop and for a while stacked shelves in Gateways Supermarket. On the application form for each job, in the box headed 'Educational Qualifications' Matt had simply written, Not Applicable. He wasn't scared of hard work and was keen to learn a trade but wherever he went they only wanted short-term cheap labour. After applying to join the Junior Leaders Regiment of the Royal Engineers he failed the physical test by one pull up, his run was in a good time, sit ups and push ups met the statutory requirements as with everything else, but he could only manage two out of the three pull ups to the bar. There was no way the examiner was going to make an exception; they would not allow him into the British Army. Disappointed, Matt applied to join the RAF as a chef in May 1987 as there was no physical entrance test, but they were only taking entrants on a YTS Scheme. It was the MOD's cunning plan to recruit, train and employ servicemen but only have to pay them a fraction of the wages a regular serviceman would receive. Matt joined anyway and eventually was taken on as a regular RAF serviceman on his first posting to RAF Honnington; this was just three months after passing his Basic and Trade training. He must have impressed someone.

Matt deployed on the first Gulf War with 20 Squadron RAF regiment (The infantry of the RAF), he catered in a field kitchen for those who had deployed but was returned to the UK before the war ended as too many cooks were spoiling the broth. He received a Gulf War medal but felt he didn't deserve it; he was overwhelmed with a sense of guilt for returning to the UK and leaving his friends in the front line. A vacancy became available in the RAF's MCSU (Mobile Catering Support Unit) and Matt was selected to fill the post. MCSU could deploy anywhere in the world and cater for any RAF unit serving in the field on Operations or Exercises. It was a job that Matt loved and with good reason, over the next few years he was lucky enough to travel to Sardinia, Norway, Denmark, Spain, and the good old US of A. Before he finished his time in the RAF he also managed to squeeze in two 6-month tours of Belize in Central America, on one of the tours he lived with a lady of ill repute who worked at Raul's Rose Garden. Among other things, she also did Matt's laundry for him and Airport

Camp's Ration Store, of which Matt had the key, paid for it all. After twelve years the RAF refused to let Matt sign on for any further service as they had a glut of Chefs, bizarrely though, they were still recruiting and training Airmen in that trade.

It was around this time that Harry divorced Ronnie and Matt briefly stayed in the empty matrimonial house in Bridlington with his girlfriend Kirsty, they were married a year later and Harry was honoured to be Matt's Best Man at the wedding. Harry also wangled a job interview for Matt as a chef in the Officers' Mess at the Defence School of Transport in Leconfield, his skills and experience in the RAF easily got him the job. They moved into their own home in Driffield and Matt joined Harry's old TA unit, 250 Field Ambulance RAMC, in Wenlock Barracks Hull. During the interview the recruiting staff tried to coerce Matt into becoming a unit chef because of his vast experience in catering, but Matt insisted that he wanted to be a medic. He'd had enough of cooking during the day, he didn't want to do it all weekend as well. He did the course at Keogh Barracks in Ash Vale and became a Combat Medical Technician and a year later passed his Class Two examination and was promoted to Lance Corporal.

Sadly, for many reasons, Matt's and Kirsty's marriage started to break down after only one year and Matt moved into a one bedroom flat in Hull opposite Wenlock Barracks. It was January 2003 and the British Army was again mobilising for war in the Middle East to sort out Saddam Hussein once and for all. There was a shortfall of most trades in the Task Force deploying on the Second Gulf War; and paradoxically for Matt, the one trade they didn't want from 250 Field Ambulance was chefs, they wanted medics, and lots of them. Matt was going back out to the Middle

27

East and this time he wouldn't be coming home early, he also wouldn't be spending his time frying eggs.

Sergeant Ritchie John
Royal Army Dental Corps
(Regular Army)
Dental Clerical Assistant Class 1

First Gulf War – 8 January 1991 to 4 April 1991

When you meet Ritchie for the very first time he appears somewhat guarded, he will not allow anyone into his personal inner sanctum until he has weighed him or her up. He doesn't suffer fools and indolent people gladly. That's not to say he isn't friendly, because he certainly is, but he has to be sure of all the facts before he will call you a 'Mate'. He describes himself as opinionated and self-confident; he also has a quiet determination to improve every aspect of his personal and professional life.

He has an endless bundle of energy bound up in a muscular frame; his swarthy good looks have always attracted beautiful women to him like bees to a honey pot. (Authors note: I hate him). He also has a very dry sense of humour and you are never sure if he is taking the piss out of you or not. (Authors note: If his lips are moving, he is taking the piss out of you). Ritchie will give you an honest opinion to any question, but if you don't want to hear the answer, then don't ask the question in the first place.

Ritchie's dad was born and raised in the small coastal town of Gouyave on the Caribbean Island of Grenade. He immigrated to England in 1958 and was quickly conscripted into the British Army for two years and served in the RCT (Royal Corps of Transport) as a Driver. He was posted out to the Middle East and whilst serving in Tripoli Garrison he met his wife to be, Ellen, who was stationed there as a QARANC (Queen Alexandra's Royal Army Nursing Corps) nurse. Ellen originally came from Glenarm Co Antrim in Northern Ireland. After returning to the UK on completion of their National Service they were married in London.

Ritchie's older brother Patrick came along in 1960 and Ritchie followed five years later on 24 November 1965; they grew up in and around Hayes Middlesex West London.

After achieving a handful of O levels at school including Maths, English, Geography, History and Religious Education, Ritchie went to the Army Careers Office to enlist into the British Army. He didn't have a clue what he wanted to do or which branch of the army did what. Patrick was already serving in the RAMC as an Environmental Health Technician but Ritchie didn't want to copy anything his brother did. After completing his initial tests the Recruiting Sergeant told Ritchie every trade in the British Army was open to him, several weeks later as he left home for the two-day selection process at Sutton Coldfield, he remembers hearing the record 'Every breath you take' by Police, blaring on someone's radio.

At Sutton Coldfield the potential recruits watched lots of films showing soldiers skiing, driving tanks and parachuting out of RAF C 130 Hercules aircraft. Every wall at the selection centre was covered in posters demonstrating just about every Branch and Trade in the British Army. Ritchie had decided he wanted a technical trade and noticed two posters on the wall next to him; one was of a Royal Artillery Gunner working on a Rapier Anti Aircraft Missile system, and the other, a Royal Army Dental Corps Dental Technician making some false teeth. The one factor that swayed Ritchie towards the life of a 'Tooth Fairy' in the British Army was the fact that the Dental Technician was working in a nice warm laboratory, and the Rapier Anti

Aircraft Controller was working outside in a Cold damp field. Ritchie didn't want to be cold or get his hands dirty, so it was the RADC (Royal Army Dental Corps) for him.

RADC soldiers undertake their Basic Training alongside RAMC recruits at the RAMC Depot near Ash Vale just outside Aldershot Garrison. The physical training was about the only part of Basic Training that Ritchie enjoyed, weapons, NBC, First Aid and all the bullshit, screaming and shouting by the instructors just pissed him off. He also hated having to get out of bed early in the morning, the instructors wanted everyone shit, showered and shaved, Block Jobs (Toilet and room cleaning) completed and on Parade for 0755 hours. Ritchie couldn't understand why it wasn't possible to do everything at a more civilised time like 1000 hours. Every recruit had to pass a BFT (Basic Fitness Test) run of three miles, one and a half miles in 15 minutes running in a squad formation, followed immediately by a second lap of the same distance to be completed in less than 11 minutes. The second lap had to be completed as an individual. Ritchie was the fastest of all the recruits on his course and felt elated when his instructors congratulated him.

When Ritchie went on his first block leave he was immensely proud of what he had achieved, he was now a trained soldier and says, "To be quite honest, I felt like the dogs bollocks." He went to the RADC Depot at Evelyn Woods Road in Aldershot for three months to complete his trade training as a Dental Clerical Assistant, in short, this meant he was going to be a Dental Nurse who could do a bit of typing. In RAMC parlance he was a 'Gob Doctor'.

Ritchie's first posting as a 'Gob Doctor' was to 19 Field Ambulance RAMC where he worked in Colchester Garrison

Dental Centre, but he also had to deploy with the Field Ambulance every time they went on Military Exercises. This rather upset his plans of staying in the warm and not getting his hands dirty. Three years later he was posted as a Lance Corporal to the Headquarters of 5 Dental Group RADC at Mill Hill, where he worked as an admin clerk until he was promoted to Corporal and posted to the Dental Centre at Pirbright.

Pirbright is the Depot and Training Division of the Brigade of Guards. All Guards recruits destined for the Coldstream, Grenadier, Scots, Irish or Welsh Guards Battalions went through Basic Training at Pirbright. The Guards Battalions do not have a rank of Full Corporal, any Corps soldiers working at the Depot of that rank, are deemed to be a Lance Sergeant and must live in the Sergeant's Mess. You have to bear in mind that in the late 1980's the Guards Division was very bigoted against any soldier who had a skin Colour that was darker than a pale shade of white.

After reporting to the Depot a Colour Sergeant who was allocating rooms to all the recently arrived soldiers disdainfully asked Ritchie, "Are you a Substantive Full Corporal?" To which Ritchie replied, "Yes Colour." The Colour Sergeant went and had a chat with some other Guards SNCOs and came back to Ritchie and sneered, "Are you sure you not an acting Full Corporal, you're positive you have Substantive Full Corporal rank?" Again Ritchie replied, "Yes Colour Sergeant, I am a Substantive Full Corporal which makes me an equivalent rank of Lance Sergeant." This gave the Colour Sergeant a massive problem because he and all the other gormless Guards SNCOs did not want a black soldier in their Mess. He solved the problem by telling Ritchie there were no rooms available in the Sergeant's Mess and allocated Ritchie a bed space in the filthy transit block.

It was unrealistic for anyone to be permanently accommodated in the sub standard transit block, so Ritchie started sleeping on a bed in the Medical Centre. This was fine until the SMO (Senior Medical Officer), who held the rank of Major, spotted all Ritchie's kit and asked why he was sleeping in there. Ritchie put him in the picture and the SMO said "Right, I'm going to have this out with the RSM, we'll soon see who can and can't be accommodated in the Sergeant's Mess!" The Major gave the RSM a bollocking that he would never forget and told him to arrange for Ritchie to be allocated a room in the Sergeant's Mess immediately. The RSM fearfully agreed to sort the whole thing out and looked at Ritchie and said, "Well, I suppose he's not that black really."

Ritchie received some curious glances from the Mess Staff as he moved all his kit into his allocated room. On his first night Ritchie went into the Mess Bar for a quick pint and all conversation in the bar stopped after he walked in. He said to the young Guardsman who was acting as barman, "I would like a pint of lager please." Knowing the Guards dislike of black servicemen, the barman was confused that Ritchie was in the bar and asking to be served like all the other white Guards Depot SNCO's. The barman turned towards the senior mess member for reassurance that it was OK for this non-white person to be served a drink. Ritchie said, "Don't look at him, I'm a mess member here, now please get me that pint of lager." Ritchie sat on a stool next to the bar and quietly drank his pint of lager; his presence seemed to have magically affected everyone's power of speech within the room. Ritchie says "To be fair once they got used to me and realised that I wasn't defiling their cap badge by wearing it on my beret, they tolerated me."

Ritchie discovered the delights of German lager and frauleins after being promoted to Sergeant and posted to BAOR. He gorged himself on both. Although Ritchie was having a great time drinking and having sex, he also continued with his strict regime of physical exercise at the end of every day. He travelled from the Sergeant's Mess in Hameln to Detmold Garrison to spend the odd weekend at the authors Married Quarter, a time badly needed, to slow down, and recharge his batteries. The day-to-day mundane existence of running a Dental Centre started to make Ritchie bolshie, he couldn't stand the majority of inept and petty minded officers he had to work for. He tried his luck on a commissioning board in an attempt to become an Officer in the British Army, there was no way he could be any worse a leader of men than some of the clowns he had served under. The board gave Ritchie a good report but said he had just failed to make the grade, Ritchie made the decision to leave the British Army and signed off. He would see out his last twelve months in the army working, or rather not working, at the Dental Centre in Osnabruck.

Colonel Jeffries RADC informed Ritchie that he was posting him to 3 AFA (Armoured Field Ambulance) for the duration of the escalating conflict in the Middle East. Ritchie pointed out to the Colonel that he had signed off and had only months to do before becoming a bona fide civilian, it would be unfair to post him out to a war zone when his time in the army was limited and anyway, he'd never really enjoyed army life. The Colonel told Ritchie that he understood the reasons why he should not be posted out to the Gulf but he was going to post him there anyway. He told Ritchie, "Let's chalk this one up to experience Sergeant John."

It looked like Ritchie was going to carry on the family tradition of serving in the ranks of the British Army, out in the Middle East. The only difference was, Ritchie was doing it with a lot of bad grace.

WAR STORIES

Corporal Mick Killeen RAMC

Mick never, ever thought he would go to war. If it did happen though, he wouldn't shirk his duty. The Territorial Army had paid him for years to attend Weekend Exercises and Training Nights in Barracks, if it came to it, he had an obligation to pay back for what he had taken. Jean interrogated him after every Drill Night he attended at Wenlock Barracks, "Has anyone said if you're going to get called up for Iraq?" It was the same answer every time, "No! It's never been mentioned; anyway the Government will reach a diplomatic solution before they ever have to resort to calling out the Territorial Army." They had been told that if they were going to be called up the notification would come through the post straight from the Ministry of Defence. Every day Jean dreaded a buff coloured envelope arriving through the letterbox telling her husband that his country needed him. It never arrived and she started to think that maybe Mick was right; when Mick came home from work one night he asked if there was any mail for him. She said, "Only that large white envelope, it's probably from the insurance company." Mick opened the letter and went pale as he started to read the full package of documentation, "What's the matter, what is it?" Jean asked nervously. Mick's reply was short and succinct, "I've been called up."

Captain Sharon Anthony QARANC

The Training Officer at 250 Field Ambulance had missed the January 2003 weekend Exercise because he had to attend an O Group at 5 GS (General Support) Medical Regiment RAMC. In recent years 250 Field Ambulance had been affiliated to 5 GS and were now called B Squadron, Hull (250), 5 GS Medical Regiment RAMC, and in the event of deploying they would make up the numbers of the Preston based Regular Army unit. The TA officers and soldiers of 250 Field Ambulance would never deploy as a Hull TA entity.

After Sharon briefed the Training Officer on her evaluation of the weekend Exercise he told her he had been, "Putting 250 Field Ambulance people into 5 GS gaps in preparation for their deployment out to Iraq." He continued, "Sharon, when you get your call up papers…" Sharon was taken aback and quickly asked, "What do you mean 'when' I get my call up papers. Does that mean I am definitely going out to Iraq?" He started back peddling immediately, "No, no, that's not what I said Sharon, I meant 'If' you get your call up papers!" Sharon didn't believe him, "You explicitly said 'When' I get my papers, not 'If'!" Sharon left the office twenty minutes later after being fully briefed by the Training Officer on what would happen 'If' she got her call up papers.

Lance Corporal Matt Fairclough RAMC

A TA soldier is limited to the amount of days he can work within his unit; the rules are governed by the budgetary cost of paying his wages. Territorial soldier's can work full time but must be on a yearly contract, which is regulated by the Ministry of Defence. Staff Sergeant Dave Horsefall RAMC was one of the Territorial senior ranks at 250 Field Ambulance who had signed up for an annual contract. Dave was Matt's boss at Wenlock Barracks and he tried to get Matt as many working days in the unit as he could. Matt needed the money and Dave needed a keen worker to sort out the units' NBC (Nuclear Biological and Chemical) equipment store, the situation suited both their needs. Matt was working on Friday afternoon and up to his knees in NBC suits, gloves and over-boots when Dave walked into the store, he was trying to arrange for some TA medics from within the unit, to provide medical cover for an up and coming two week training exercise. 22 SAS Regiment would also be involved in the training. When Dave told Matt about the exercise Matt automatically volunteered, the chance to work in the field and possibly watch the Special Forces in action was too good an opportunity to miss. Dave told him, "You can't go Matt, you're going somewhere else soon, and you'll need a bucket and spade." Annoyingly for Matt, Dave would not elucidate on his brief remark.

On the following Monday Matt was having a cigarette with Dave in his office prior to starting the days work, they were supposed to have started at 0800 hours but it was now 0830 hours, Dave handed an envelope to Matt and said, "These are for you mate, good luck." Matt opened the envelope and read his mobilisation orders and realised he was probably going out to Iraq; he turned to Dave and said, "Can I borrow a Land Rover; I need to go and see my dad."

Sergeant Ritchie John RADC

It was on Friday afternoon when Colonel Jeffries RADC informed Ritchie that he was posting him to 3 AFA (Armoured Field Ambulance) for the duration of the Gulf War; Ritchie spent the rest of the weekend packing up his room in the Sergeant's Mess whilst muttering obscenities and chuntering about his premonitions of what serious accidents he would like to befall Colonel Jeffries. He packed all his civilian clothes and other non-essential items into some cardboard boxes and put them in the care of the RQMS at Roberts Barracks, the boxes would be securely held in the Quartermasters store until he returned. Ritchie also filled out a will and left his massive and awful record collection to be split between Corporal Jim Juby RE (Royal Engineers) and Sergeant Billy Cairns RAMC, Ritchie knew them from his days running the Dental Centre at Hameln and like him they were both Heavy Metal freaks. Everything else Ritchie possessed in the whole world, which wasn't a lot, was to be left to his mum.

At 0700 hours the following Monday morning Ritchie got on one of many coaches that were going to take him and other soldiers to Munster so they could join up with 3 AFA.

Corporal Mick Killeen RAMC

All the Medics and Drivers from the, now renamed, Hull (250) B Squadron 5 GS Medical Regiment RAMC who had been called up had to report to Chilwell for a medical examination. After successfully passing that, they were issued with the following equipment:

1. SA 80 Rifles, magazines and cleaning kit.
2. NBC suits.
3. New Respirators and extra canisters
4. NAPS (Nerve Agent Pre-treatment Set) tablets.
5. BATS (Biological Agent Treatment Set) capsules.
6. COMBO Pens (For self treatment if poisoned by Nerve Agent).
7. Body Armour.
8. Morphine Autoject Pen.
9. All old and worn Combat clothing was also replaced.

Two days later they were transported to the TA Training Centre at Grantham and spent the next five days doing intensive training in Battlefield First Aid, NBC and weapon training, which included a trip to the Ranges to zero their weapons.

Before they went to Chilwell and Grantham they were briefed in Wenlock Barracks about what they were about to face and what was expected of them. After completing his briefing, the Training Officer asked if there were any questions and one of the young female medics put her hand up and asked, "What civilian clothing can we take with us?" He pulled the collar of his combat jacket and said, "If it's not in these colours, you won't need it." It was a stupid question from a naive young TA soldier, but at least she was there, Mick had some respect for her for that. But Mick was absolutely incensed by other TA soldiers in the unit, who, on being called up put in deferments immediately. Some had decided to take up nursing training (which automatically qualified a person for exemption from call up) as soon as that large white envelope hit their doormat. Another had deferred because his firm put a case forward saying that business would be adversely affected if he deployed, what he didn't declare to the board was that he was self employed and had put up the case himself, in this type of scenario he would never be able to deploy and shouldn't have been in the TA in the first place.

At Grantham they were told all Hull (250) personnel were going to be absorbed into other sections within 5 GS (General Support) Medical Regiment RAMC, Mick was disappointed as he thought they were going to deploy as Hull (250) B Squadron RAMC. They joined up with 5 GS Medical Regiment (Rear) in the units' Barracks in Preston Lancashire, and then they were all transported down to RAF South Cerney for the flight out to Kuwait City.

Captain Sharon Anthony QARANC

The amount of Hull 250 personnel who were receiving their call up papers was increasing and some of them were from Sharon's Castleford Detachment. Sharon felt she was letting the soldiers from Castleford down and yet part of her thought 'Thank God it's not me that's going'.

On Monday evening one-week later Sharon came home from work and as she walked in the house Mick was cooking tea, "There's some mail for you," he laughed, "It might be your call up papers." It was. Sharon felt physically sick and excited at the same time, she also felt sorry for Mick because he hadn't got the chance to go out on the last Gulf War and as he had left the TA several years earlier he wouldn't be going this time either. It just didn't seem right to Sharon, their roles had been reversed, and whilst her husband was staying at home she could possibly be going off to war.

Sharon phoned Compass (the addiction services she worked for) the following day to tell them she could possibly be going to Iraq and enquired if this would result in her losing her job. She received a fax the following day giving assurance that not only would they keep a job open for her, they would put her back in exactly the same post on her safe return. She was also a bit disappointed that they could do without her so easily.

At the next Drill Night in Hull Sharon went in to Collect her Bergen and exchange her helmet for a new one, one of the units' MSO (Medical Support Officers) was effing and blinding because he hadn't been called up. Clinical staff like doctors, nurses and medics were needed to attend to the expected casualties, they didn't need glorified admin clerks. Sharon bumped into Captain Natalie Baker who explained that she also had been called up as a Nursing Officer, when Sharon pointed out the fact that Natalie hadn't done a Junior Officers Course or attended any training weekends for a while she said, "That doesn't matter, I've signed on the dotted line and the MOD have asked me to go to Iraq, so I have to go!"

Ten days after receiving their call up papers Sharon and Natalie were sent, with a whole host of other officers and soldiers, to Chilwell for a couple of days. Once there, they were subject to a thorough medical and dental examination to ensure they were all fit enough to deploy. They were given a mixture of inoculations for Hepatitis A, Hepatitis B, Smallpox, Anthrax, and Typhoid. They were also asked to fill out new Wills and were issued with body armour and weapons, Sharon was given a 9mm pistol but wasn't very confident she could hit anything with it, "I had fired the SA 80 and I could hit the target but usually in the wrong places."

Those that were deemed medically and dentally fit enough to go out to Iraq were then sent to either Grantham or Beckingham for intensive training. They were put through their paces in Vehicle recognition, Mines, NBC (Nuclear Biological and Chemical Warfare), Battlefield First Aid, weapon handling, Geneva Convention, and how to deal with the media. Sharon and all the other pupils, most of whom were highly trained and experienced medical personnel, found the Battlefield First Aid a total waste of time; in fact they spent most of the lessons correcting the instructor who was a Corporal from the Green Howard's Infantry Regiment. However, the NBC Instructor whose lessons were very interesting and amusing really impressed Sharon.

On the penultimate day of training everyone was paraded to learn which units' he or she were going to join, most of the Hull TA soldiers had already been seconded to 5 GS Medical Regiment and Sharon expected she would be joining them. The OC (Officer Commanding) of Beckingham Training Area called out names and then told them which unit they were going to join.
"Captain Baker....1 CS (Close Support) Medical Regiment RAMC." Sharon looked at Natalie in disbelief; any CS Medical unit would be serving right up in the front line. The OC's next words sent a chill down Sharon's spine, "Captain Anthony....1 CS Medical Regiment RAMC."

Lance Corporal Matt Fairclough RAMC

Matt drove the borrowed TA Land Rover from Wenlock Barracks in Hull to the Defence School of Transport in Leconfield where his dad Harry worked. Harry was surprised to see him, especially as Matt was wearing his RAMC uniform; Matt hadn't worked as a chef at Leconfield Officers Mess for at least two months but had obviously got onto the camp using his TA MOD Form 90 (Military Identity Card). The news that he had been mobilised was a shock to Harry and he told Matt that if he deployed as a medic, things might be a lot rougher than the last time he deployed as a chef with the RAF. When Harry asked if he wanted to go, Matt replied, "I don't really have a good enough reason not to go."

The following Friday Matt handed back his rented flat in Coltman Street not far from Wenlock Barracks, he told the bloke that he rented the flat from, "I've left my double bed, three piece suite, pots, pans and everything else so you can probably rent this place out now as a furnished property, I just don't have time to sell everything." The landlord seemed quite pleased with the donation of nearly new furnishings and the fact that Matt had left the place scrupulously clean. At the time, Matt was looking after a friend's flat just up the road; she was also a TA soldier and was on a CMT (Combat Medical Technician) course down at the RAMC Depot near Aldershot. Matt utilised her place for the time he had left in Hull. The soldiers who had been mobilised arranged a party in the Junior Ranks Bar at Wenlock Barracks so they could say goodbye to all their family and friends. Matt had been bought a camouflage-patterned thong as a farewell gift from a TA mate's wife, after drinking copious pints of beer he was pissed as a fart and took great pleasure in modelling the fashion item around the bar.

At 1030 hours on Monday morning; Matt and the other mobilised soldiers departed Wenlock Barracks in a coach for the journey down to Chilwell to start the mobilisation process.

Sergeant Ritchie John RADC

Ritchie joined up with 3 AFA in Munster where they were carrying out their own pre-deployment training, he was told his job within the unit would be to organise and run the CDC (Casualty Decontamination Cell). The CDC would be located at the very front of the Field Ambulance in a 12x12 tent, Ritchie and his team would be responsible for dealing with any casualties that were contaminated with chemical agents. This role was always carried out in Field Ambulance units by soldiers of the RADC (Royal Army Dental Corps), they would check for any chemical contamination on the casualties NBC suits using detector papers and CAM's (Chemical Agent Monitors). A CAM is an army green coloured and hand held device not dissimilar to a household dust buster; it vacuum's up chemical vapours and identifies the saturation level of the chemical agent present on an LCD. The tent they worked in would be divided into two areas, each with trestles that a stretcher could be placed onto, plastic white mining tape segregated the areas, one side was clean, and the other was dirty. The casualty would be received into the dirty area and decontaminated using Fullers earth (exactly the same stuff as the makeup that women put on their faces from a powder compact) and his NBC suit, gloves and boots would be cut off and put into a gas proof bag ready for disposal. The casualty's respirator would be decontaminated but not removed and he would at this stage have any wounds, and dressings checked; the casualty would then be lifted over the clean/dirty line and onto the clean stretcher ready to be taken about fifty meters up to the Field Ambulance Reception area where his medical treatment could begin. It should be possible to decontaminate and prep one casualty every twenty minutes; but carrying out this role, even in mid winter in Germany, is ball-breaking work and of course each soldier working in the CDC would be sweating his bollocks off because they would be working in full NBC suits. Ritchie had carried out this role on Exercise many times when he was attached to 19 Field Ambulance in Colchester Garrison. To assist him in the CDC, Ritchie was given four other RADC soldiers who were a mixture of Lance Corporals and Privates, if working in a CDC was hot work in temperate climates, Ritchie wondered what the hell it was going to be like in the Saudi desert.

Corporal Mick Killeen RAMC

The fact that the French Government was opting out of the 'war against terrorism' really annoyed Mick, everyone was at risk and he thought, "Them bastards should be doing their bit alongside the rest of us." That was bad enough but when he saw the plane that was going to fly them out to the Middle East was a French Corsair 747 airliner, he felt personally aggrieved. "They weren't prepared to fight alongside us but were happy to make money out of chartering their aircraft to fly the British Army out to the war zone." He felt that it just wasn't right.

He phoned Jean on his mobile as they all started to troop out of the departure lounge. Jean was picking up the toys that were scattered around her back garden, the kids that she child minded everyday had made a mess and she was clearing everything away now they had all gone home. She answered her mobile phone as she tidied the garden and heard Mick tell her he was ringing to say goodbye, he seemed to be really choked up and on the verge of crying. Jean instantly became emotional herself and tried very hard to hold back the tears.

Jean: "Where are you going?"

47

Mick: "Iraq."

Jean: "Well how long are you going to be there?"

Mick: "I don't know."

Jean: "Well guess, will it be more than a month?"

Mick: "It's going to be for a long time."

The phone connection went dead and Jean thought 'that might be the last time I ever speak to my Mick, what will I tell Rachel and Victoria'? It would be three weeks before she got her first letter from Mick.

Captain Sharon Anthony QARANC

On completion of their training at Beckingham all the officers and soldiers were either sent back to Strensall and Birmingham or they went to 5 GS Medical Regiment RAMC (Rear) to await travel orders to join the Regiment out in Kuwait. Sharon and Natalie accompanied several others on a minibus that took them straight to South Cerney so they could catch a flight out to Kuwait that night. When they arrived at South Cerney they were put up in the Officers' Mess as the flight had been cancelled and they wouldn't be flying for another two days. Sharon and Mick decided on the telephone not to tell their children, family, and friends about the fact she was going to join 1 CS Medical Regiment RAMC. Mick thought the severity of danger Sharon was going to be put in need not be told to everyone, they would keep that little secret to themselves. Sharon wrote individual letters and put them in sealed envelopes addressed to Mick, the kids and her other close family members. All the letters were put in a large jiffy envelope and sent to her friend in Hornsea who would distribute them if the unthinkable happened.

Two days later coach loads of officers and soldiers arrived at Brize Norton ready to check in for flights out to Kuwait, Sharon would be flying at 2000 hours on an Icelandic 747 that had been chartered by the MOD, that night was Sharon's wedding anniversary. Once the flight was airborne she started talking to an RLC Driver who was within the last month of his time in the army and the MOD saw no reason why he shouldn't go to Iraq with everyone else. He was not a happy bunny.

After landing at Kuwait Airport and taxiing to the airport terminal, the pilot addressed his passengers but clearly forgot exactly who he was carrying, "We have now landed at Kuwait Airport, please make sure you take all your hand luggage with you and on behalf of Air Iceland we hope you have a great holiday and look forward to...Oh shit...sorry about that....I mean, good luck and I hope you all get back safe and sound."

Everyone on board cheered the clearly embarrassed pilot.

Lance Corporal Matt Fairclough RAMC

Not every TA soldier who arrived at Chilwell for mobilisation was fit enough to be sent out to Iraq, some had been turned down for seemingly inessential reasons. A Sapper from 131 Independent Commando Squadron RE (Royal Engineers) was rejected because he was dentally unfit and the treatment involved to get him fit would have been costly and lengthy. The paradox of the whole situation was that as a Commando trained soldier he was probably physically fitter than any of the medics who had been passed satisfactory.

The soldiers who passed the dental and medical examinations were then issued all the extra equipment needed for their operational tour. This included weapons, and bizarrely the medics were also issued bayonets for their SA 80 rifles. Medics shouldn't be issued bayonets under the rules of the Geneva Convention because as troops, they are never involved in an attacking role, Matt pointed this out to the armourer at Chilwell but was told, "It doesn't matter, just take it out to Kuwait with you and they will withdraw it off you out there and probably give it to someone else." In the tabloid press some weeks earlier a TA female medic was photographed holding an SA 80, with bayonet attached, and pictured standing in an aggressive pose. The press can easily persuade unwitting soldiers into doing these stupid things with the promise of giving them fifteen minutes of fame. She and her unit press officer really should have known better though.

Matt and his fellow medics went to Grantham for five days intensive training in various military subjects before joining up with 5 GS Medical Regiment RAMC (Rear) at their base in Preston. On arrival at Preston they handed personal weapons into the armoury for their couple of days stay over, they certainly wouldn't need rifles for the medical lectures from 5 GS instructors on wound management. Also, they couldn't realistically go on the piss in the pub over the road at night carrying rifles; soldiers, weapons and excessive alcohol are not a good mix at any time or in any place. The 5 GS Medical Regiment armourer was amazed that they, as medics, had been issued with bayonets and said they wouldn't be re-issued to them when they drew weapons before leaving the barracks. The unit would have a quiet word in the ear of the staff at Chilwell to make sure they didn't issue them to any other medics that came through the system.

Two days later Matt and the other medics headed off to South Cerney for the flight out to Kuwait on a French 747 airliner that was only half full, the good parts of the flight were, the airhostesses were gorgeous and the fact that Matt had four seats in which to stretch out and sleep on. The bad part of the flight was the in flight food, they were served a French dish of fish and rice, and as a qualified chef, Matt felt he was well within his rights to call it, "French shit!" Matt slept for most of the flight out to Kuwait.

Sergeant Ritchie John RADC

Ritchie spent four weeks in Munster with 3 AFA doing some CDC training with his new team and spent most of his free time at Staff Sergeant Bob Darkin's Married Quarter flat. Bob was an old friend of Ritchie's from his days at Pirbright where Ritchie ran the Dental Centre and Bob was one of the medics who worked in the Medical Centre. Bob was also deploying with 3 AFA as the Dressing Station Acting Staff Sergeant. He was temporarily filling in the post and wore the rank of Staff Sergeant (Staff Sergeant- Three stripes with a crown above it) because no one had been permanently posted in to fill the vacancy. The unit was called back to Sennelager Training area, 3 AFA's home base, to begin four weeks supervised training in NBC, First Aid, PT and a multitude of other military subjects, Staff Sergeant Bob Darkin described the training as "Dull as ditch water." In one of the lectures about aircraft recognition Ritchie whispered in Bob's ear, "Why do we have to do this, we won't be able to shoot anything down?" Bob growled, "Just shut up and get on with it." As they looked at even more

51

slides and posters of military aircraft Ritchie wouldn't let it go, "But Bob, those are Soviet aircraft with Soviet Air Force markings on them, what use is this going to be to us?" Bob's reply was terse, "Will you fucking shut up and just get on with it!"

On completion of their training programme at Sennelager, Ritchie and the other soldiers of 3 AFA headed off to Hanover airport to catch their flight out to Saudi Arabia.

Corporal Mick Killeen RAMC

As the doors of the 747 airliner opened after landing at Kuwait City Airport, Mick was struck by how hot it was after leaving the air-conditioned environment of the aircraft. "It was like walking into a furnace" said Mick as he described the oppressive heat. It seemed to take forever to find his kit amongst a mountain of baggage; unfortunately all the other passengers on his flight seemed to have packed their holiday clothing in similar suitcases, a DPM 150 Litre Bergen. A sand storm had just started and was making the job of finding his kit even harder. They all went through a military reception area at the airport and Mick swiped his ID card through a Bar Coding machine that officially registered him with the MOD as arriving in the country.

All the new arrivals were herded onto trucks and taken up to one of the Eagle Camps which was about an hours drive from the Iraq border. On the journey Mick noticed the side of the road was lined with the longest and highest wire garden fence he had ever seen in his life. It was, presumably, there to stop any unaccompanied camels from strolling onto the highway and ending up like many a hedgehog does in the UK. The entire fence only seemed to stop and collect hundreds and hundreds of plastic carrier bags.

At the Eagle Camp they at last caught up with 5 GS Medical Regiment (Main) as another horrendous sand storm was starting and visibility was reduced to about 2 meters. Mick describes it thus, "Everyone calls it a sand storm but it is more like a dust storm, it's similar to standing in thick fog, only in this case the fog gets in your eyes and up your nostrils." Mick was allocated a space in a large Arabian Army marquee type tent to live in with Corporal Mick Pallister, Sergeant Paul Greensides, Sergeant Roberts (all three were RAMC and from Hull 250) and several other 'new boys'. The marquee was divided in two with accommodation space for thirty soldiers on one side and the other used as an admin area. As the wind outside battered the sides of the tent Mick felt like a five year old on his first day at school, he needed his friends by his side to make him feel safe and secure.

Eagle camp was a gigantic tented city and Mick was surprised they hadn't had a welcome speech from an officer saying, "Welcome to Kuwait, this promises to be a challenging Exercise, make the most of the weekends training and we will all have a beer in the bar at Wenlock Barracks on Sunday afternoon." There wasn't a cookhouse, there wasn't even any food, and no one seemed to be interested in him or his welfare. When Mick received his first meal, apart from the US Forces MRE (Meals Ready to Eat) Ration Packs they were given shortly after arrival, it was from a Hay Box and consisted of a green stew, during the entire war there was a menu of green, brown or red stew. You could only differentiate the stews by colour, as they all tasted the same. It was starting to dawn on Mick that he was now on a war footing.

53

Captain Sharon Anthony QARANC

On arrival at Kuwait Airport Sharon and the other new arrivals were given a long list of contraband, which included pornography and alcohol, which were prohibited on entry to Kuwait. All baggage would be searched after they had left the aircraft. Veronica, who was also from 250 Field Ambulance, suddenly whispered in Sharon's ear, "Shit! I've got a loaded magazine in my hand luggage." Somewhat shocked Sharon replied, "How the hell did you manage to get that through the security checks at Brize Norton. What are you going to do with it?" With a worried look on her face Veronica said "There are some skips over there, I'll just throw it into one of them." "You can't throw a fully loaded magazine into a skip, you'll have to unload it and hand the ammunition into the Quartermasters Department" suggested Sharon. Even more confused Veronica said, "What are you talking about? I haven't got any ammunition; I meant I've got a magazine called Loaded in my hand luggage!"

Lance Corporal Matt Fairclough RAMC

It was dawn when Matt arrived at Kuwait City airport, the sun was only half way up in the sky but he could already feel the heat from the sun as they opened the aircraft doors. After collecting his Bergen, weapon and webbing he waited in the long line of arrivals to go through the arrival documentation process, once his ID card had been electronically swiped and he was registered with the MOD as being 'In Theatre', he stood to one side with all the other processed soldiers and awaited the transport that would take him up to the Eagle Camp where5 GS Medical Regiment was based.

An American soldier who was involved in the US Army processing system came over to chat with the newly arrived 'Brits', "Hey guys, I've been working with you fella's for a while now, and I know that you call cigarettes, 'fags', in the States we call homosexuals 'fags'. I was really worried when one Brit soldier came up to me and asked me if he could, "Bum an American fag off me." Is there any chance I could bum an English fag off one of you guys?" Matt bummed him a Benson and Hedges. As the grateful American smoked Matt's cigarette he pointed out the plethora of ISO shipping containers scattered around the airport, they were banked up at the sides with sand and the tops were covered in filled sandbags, "If you hear a missile alarm just head for the containers, they are our shelters in the event of a Scud Missile attack."

Sergeant Ritchie John RADC

Ritchie sat next to Sergeant Bob Darkin on the flight out to Saudi Arabia even though the Air Kuwait Boeing 747 was only carrying about half the passengers it was capable of transporting, there was plenty of room to spread themselves out and get some sleep on the seven hour flight. They took off from Hanover airport at 0200 hours and landed at about 0900 hours. After getting off the plane Ritchie walked the short distance from the aircraft steps to the Admin Hangar. Because of the intense heat Ritchie describes it as, "The most exhausting walk of my life, it was absolutely boiling hot when we arrived." Once in the Hangar everyone in the unit had to fill in several forms giving information about their Next of **Kin and blood group, despite having given this information before** leaving Germany, at the same time Dog Tags were distributed to all the soldiers in the unit. These Identity Discs comprise of two metals discs worn around the neck on a piece of cord and they contain a soldiers' serial number, rank, name, religion and blood group, in the event of a soldier being killed one disc remains on the body and the other is given to his unit to notify them of his death.

The enormity of everything astounded Ritchie; the airport was a hive of activity and home to Military and civilian aeroplanes of all sizes, helicopters, tanks, trucks and hundreds of service personnel running hither and thither. Once the unit had been processed through the admin set up in the hangar, they were herded onto some US Air Force yellow 'Freddie Kruger' style buses that would take them to an American run military camp, the Yanks at the camp fed Ritchie and his mates a very decent meal. After getting back on the bus they were each given a bottle of water and told to keep drinking because the risk of dehydration causing heat exhaustion and heat stroke injuries was a very real possibility. The Arab driver of the bus was playing Arabic style music on his ghetto blaster whilst everyone on the bus sat silently watching the desert go by. The bus was taking them to a British Army tented city called Baldrick Lines where they would be accommodated.

Corporal Mick Killeen RAMC

Whilst Mick was training at Grantham before deploying out to the Gulf, he and his mates from 250 left all pre packed main Bergen's in the store at Wenlock Barracks. They collected them before travelling out to join 5 GS Medical Regiment in the desert. At the Eagle Camp Mick was delving into his Bergen trying to find something or other when he felt something metallic that he hadn't packed at the bottom, he pulled out a large electric metal fan with a note tied onto it. Private Jamie Flatt RLC was a cook in 250 and had not been mobilised, he broke into the store and packed the fan into Mick's Bergen. The note read 'Mick, if it gets too hot in the desert, here is a fan for you'. Mick didn't know whether to laugh or cry.

Captain Sharon Anthony QARANC

It was 0600 hours when Sharon arrived at Kuwait Airport and as she looked at about thee hundred Bergen's and sets of webbing she wondered how on earth she was going to find her own. The RAF Movements Clerks at Brize Norton, for reasons known only to them, insisted that any identification tags, strings, or labels had to be removed before they were loaded onto the aircraft. As she and hundreds of other arrivals pondered the same problem everyone in the hangar heard a booming voice shout, "CAPTAIN ANTHONY! GET YOUR BIG FAT ARSE OVER HERE NOW!" It was Captain John Batcock RAMC who had come to pick up all the medical personnel destined for 1 CS Medical Regiment, Sharon knew him from old when he was the Training Officer at 250 Field Ambulance in Hull. She was pleased to see a familiar and friendly albeit abusive face. He told her "I've been looking forward to you getting here ever since I saw your name on 1 CS's nominal roll." Reassuringly he said, "Don't worry Sharon, we'll look after you."

Sharon loaded her kit into a long wheel based Land Rover and they headed off to Coyote Camp where Headquarters 1 CS Medical Regiment was based. They were met in the Mess tent by the Commanding Officer who shook everyone's hand and asked their names, he then went on to brief them on the current situation and 1 CS's role when the fighting actually started. 1 CS Medical Regiment would be supporting an Armoured Brigade consisting of 2 RTR (Royal Tank Regiment), the SDG (Scots Dragoon Guards) and 1st Battalion of the Irish Guards, two Dressing Stations would be set up behind the Collecting Sections who would deploy just behind the fighting troops. All the officers were asked to list their qualifications and medical experience so they could be placed in the most appropriate department within the unit. Sharon thought her experience of 'Working with substance abuse patients' would be of no use to anyone on a battlefield and presumed she would be put into a supporting role in one of the Dressing Stations. She couldn't believe what she was hearing when the appointments were read out, "Captain Anthony... you will be OIC (Officer in Charge) of the Collecting Section supporting the Scots Dragoon Guard's Armoured Regiment."

Lance Corporal Matt Fairclough RAMC

Matt was assigned to Juliet Troop of 5 GS Medical Regiment RAMC; the other two Crewmembers on his allocated ambulance were Private 'Murph' Murphy, a Regular Army CMT 1 who was appointed Crew Commander, and the Driver was an Irish TA RLC Lance Corporal, who was transferred in to the unit from the Air Assault Brigade and came wearing an airborne maroon beret the Air Assault Quartermaster had given him to wear. He was told to "Get that fucking thing off your head and start wearing a bush hat or helmet, you are with 5 GS Medical Regiment now!" Unimaginatively, Matt and 'Murph' called him 'Paddy'.

The three of them started preparing their allocated and empty ambulance with all the equipment required for the war ahead. They had never seen so much equipment and what was dumped at the rear of their ambulance was just for them. Apart from the obvious kit like stretchers, there were no instructions on where to put the rest of the paraphernalia.

All electrical gizmos were situated next to the stretcher so they could be used on the main casualty, but the spare O2 bottles, Jerry cans of water, Webbing, Bergen's, Rations, Picks, shovels and camp beds, etc also had to be found a home within their new mobile medical facility. The problem was that the ambulance wasn't designed to carry it all.

There were two rifle racks in the front of the ambulance to store the Crew Commanders and Drivers weapons and two in the rear of the ambulance to store the medic's weapon and the casualty they were conveying, but, if they were carrying one prone and three sitting casualties "God only knew where we were going put their weapons let alone their sets of webbing and Bergen's", states Matt. The sole instruction given by 5 GS Medical Regiment was, "The only gear to be carried on the outside of the vehicle is the spare wheel on the roof, along with the canvas shelter and poles for use by the crew when laagered up, some camp beds may be bungeed on the ambulance bonnet." The reason for these restrictions was made clear on a briefing, the ambulances were top heavy, and if you were to put extra hardware on the top or around the outside of the vehicle, it would very easily roll over when travelling over uneven ground. Matt and his crew members never used the canvas shelter because it was too time consuming to pack up when given a shout to collect casualties; it remained unopened on the roof of their ambulance throughout the entire war.

Every member of the crew had to get their own personal admin sorted out before they actually went to war, to say to a casualty, "Sorry mate, I'll just shift these dirty mess tins out of the way before I can start putting a cannula into the vein in your arm" would have been embarrassing and unprofessional to say the least. Good husbandry and cleanliness is drummed into all British Army soldiers during

Basic Training and is the minimum standard required when living in crowded and cramped conditions, for the medics with their limited space it was going to be essential.

Sergeant Ritchie John RADC

When Ritchie arrived at Baldrick Lines and was allocated a tent to sleep in, his first comment to Staff Sergeant Bob Darkin was, "Bloody hell mate! This is a fucking dump." To which Bob replied, "Will you stop fucking moaning!" As far as the eye could see there was row upon row of British Army tents lined up as if they were taking part in a Trooping of the Colours Parade in London. Each tent was empty of any creature comforts, not even a camp bed was provided. Ritchie needn't have worried though because the unit were not going to hang around in Baldrick Lines for very long, the very next day everyone was taken to the docks at Al Jubayl to pick up the units' vehicles and medical equipment. The 3 AFA Land Rovers and 4 tonners had been sent out to Saudi Arabia weeks before the unit had even started their training at Sennelager, the medical equipment had also been sent on ahead in a shipping container after it had all been checked over at D Med (Defence Medical Equipment Depot) in Bielefeld. As they travelled down to the docks in army trucks Bob Darkin explained to Ritchie that their particular equipment was in a massive green shipping container and he was in possession of the only padlock key that would open it.

When they arrived at the docks Bob and Ritchie were confronted by, literally, hundreds and hundreds of green shipping containers and the port authorities were unsure which one was 3 AFA's, Bob realised it was going to take forever and a day to find their particular container; he summed up his feelings in one word… "Bollocks!"

Corporal Mick Killeen RAMC

The TA soldiers from 250 Field Ambulance were split up and distributed around 5 GS Medical Regiment and Mick was assigned to one of the British Army's latest designed Land Rover ambulances. All RAMC ambulances during the second Gulf War operated in pairs and each had a crew of three on board, the crew commander, an RLC (Royal Logistic Corps) driver and obviously, a medic in the back of the vehicle. Mick was told he was going to be one of those medics. The Crew Commander was a TA RAMC Corporal called Derek who, in his civilian life, was an Ambulance Paramedic with a Cambridgeshire Health Trust. Mick describes the RLC driver as "The bravest little bastard I have ever met in my life." Private Yasser Naseem was a 19-year-old Regular Army soldier whose parents came from a little village in Pakistan but now lived in Bolton Lancashire. If the Iraqi Army caught a Muslim soldier serving in the British Army, the consequences were unthinkable. Yasser was the absolute spitting image of the World Champion Featherweight Boxer Prince Hamed Naseem; so much so, that when Mick met Yasser for the first time he thought he actually was Prince Hamed.

The three of them spent the next eight days preparing their chariot for war, they had to sort out the radio equipment, and camouflage nets for the ambulance and they were also given a brand new boxed complete medical kit. There was enough kit in the box to equip a medical centre, it had spinal boards, suction apparatus, pulse oximeter, intravenous infusions and more shell dressings and bandages than you could 'shake a stick at'. Ominously they were also issued with 100 rounds of ammunition each for their personal weapons.

Captain Sharon Anthony QARANC

Sharon's Section were on exercise in the desert when she arrived so her introduction to the troops under her command would have to wait another 24 hours, she spent this time wandering around the different departments in the Main Dressing Station getting told to "Bugger off, we're busy." Feeling a bit of a spare part she was glad when a Land Rover was detailed to take her up the line and deliver her to the Section location.

The Section personnel were all Regular Army and consisted of a Sergeant CMT (Combat Medical Technician) Class 1, a 21 year old Lance Corporal CMT Class 1, and four CMT Class 2 Privates, three of which were females not older than 19 years of age. Sharon thought, 'Bloody hell, my kids are older than this lot'. The Section had two four tonners and two soft top Land Rovers and they worked out of a 12x12 tent where the casualties would be treated on stretchers placed on trestles.

On inspecting the sections equipment Sharon found some of the Privates couldn't identify certain items of kit and were unsure on how to use some of the other items. There was no loading list for the 4 tonners in the event of a move, when they did eventually move; all the medical boxes were loaded at the front of the wagon under tentage, stretchers, Bergen's, and all the other paraphernalia needed to operate a Medical Section. Sharon asked the Section Sergeant what would happen if they needed to carry out 'Tailboard Treatments' (This is when a Section receives casualties and treats their wounds without setting everything up). The Sergeant didn't appear to be very interested so over the next two days Sharon took the Section through some training and set out orders on how she wanted the wagons loaded and the procedures to follow when casualties arrived at their location. She thought, 'Flipping heck, I'm only TA, This lot are Regular Army, they should already know about these things'. A Private in Sharon's Section told her that she had spent most of her time at 1 CS Medical Regiment painting medical boxes and vehicles.

Lance Corporal Matt Fairclough RAMC

Matt's Troop Sergeant at 5 GS Medical Regiment held a Parade for all Crew Members of the four Troop ambulances; he wanted to supervise the last admin details before they went over the border into Iraq. He dished out some medium sized Jiffy bags and told everyone to put all personal documents in the bag, seal it, write on their number, rank, name and troop, and then sign the edge of the seal and hand it back to him. These envelopes would be safely stored at RHQ and returned at the end of hostilities. Documents to be included were chequebooks, bankcards, letters, and anything that could be of use to the enemy 'Military Intelligence' if they were captured. Matt put his East Yorkshire Library Card in just to be on the safe side. The only documents to be carried by soldiers in Iraq were their MOD Form 90 (Military Identity Card), FMT 600 (Military Driving Licence), and F Ident 107, which are only issued to all personnel working with the medical services. It is a buff coloured and serial numbered form that contains the details, signature and photograph of the holder of the card. If captured by the enemy the bearer of the F Ident 107 should be allowed to continue with his humanitarian work and then given safe passage back to his own lines. That is the theory anyway.

Sergeant Ritchie John RADC

When Ritchie and Bob found the right shipping container all the medical boxes, stretchers, tentage and plethora of other kit was loaded onto each department's vehicle. Every medic was also issued his personal weapon at the docks, in Ritchie's case; he was given a 9mm SMG (Sub Machine Gun) that was an updated version of the British World War Two Sten Gun. Once loaded up they returned to the tent city known as Baldrick Lines where ammunition was dished out to everyone in the unit. Ritchie was given sixty rounds of ammo which fully loaded his two magazines. The unit was also issued enough Compo Ration packs to feed themselves on their four-week acclimatisation training exercise, at the end of which Ritchie would think Baldrick Lines was a five star holiday camp. With a certain amount of trepidation Ritchie and 3 AFA headed out into the desert.

Corporal Mick Killeen RAMC

All 5 GS Medical Regiment personnel were paraded in Troop formations and ordered to take NAPS (Nerve Agent Pre-treatment Set) tablets by their respective Troop Sergeant's, the Sergeant's were to supervise and make sure everyone complied with the order. NAPS tablets provided a protective layer over nerve receptors in the human body, if Nerve Agent gets into the human body the protective layer would give the casualty extra time to self administer a Combo Pen (an injected antidote to Nerve Agent poisoning) before involuntary muscle twitching and jerking started. The tablets came in a blister pack of 21 tablets similar to the style of women's contraceptive pills. They had to be taken three times a day for a complete week.

The Sergeant stood in front of Mick and told him to go ahead and take the tablet, Mick said, "How does fuck off sound Sarge." There wasn't a list of ingredients on the package and Mick was uneasy about the possible repercussions of taking unspecified substances. If he were exposed to chemical agents, Mick would take his chances.

Captain Sharon Anthony QARANC

1 CS did a couple of days training before they were given 24 hours notice to move, the shit was about to hit the fan and the allied forces were preparing themselves to face it. Before the training had started Sharon went through her first experience of a sand storm, she had to help hold the tent down during the violent winds because the section hadn't secured it down properly.

Staff Sergeant Kenny Brown RAMC was an old school regular soldier who would kick you up the arse if you fucked up. He came into Sharon's 12x12 to take away half of everyone's ammunition for their personal weapons and their body armour. The forward troops had insufficient of both to achieve their missions and all support units had to relinquish any spare ammo for the fighting troops. Sharon felt Kenny was watching over her and her section from a distance, and because Sharon was sleeping on a stretcher; he went out of his way to purloin a camp bed so she would be more comfortable. As she handed over her body armour Kenny said, "No, you keep your body armour ma'am, you're TA not a regular, I think you should keep yours." Sharon felt very grateful for this act of kindness and said "Cheers mate."

Lance Corporal Matt Fairclough RAMC

Soldiers of the RAMC start doing their jobs immediately they arrive in a theatre of operations much like the Chefs, Vehicle Mechanics and all the other Corps that turn the mighty cogs of the British Army. The teeth arms (Infantry, Artillery, Tanks) may prepare with in-theatre training but until the shit starts hitting the fan they don't actually kill anyone, which is primarily the job they have been sent to do. The RAMC on the other hand have to start treating the sick and those injured in accidents virtually from day one. Prior to the war starting RAMC ambulances were allowed to function singularly and without an escort.

It was at this stage that Matt and his crew were dispatched to an RAMC Dressing Station to collect an American National Guard Marine and take him to a Field Hospital in Kuwait City, a round trip of eight hours. The US Marine was a 6 foot 6 inch, 19 year old, colossus of sheer muscle who had a neck the size of one of Matt's thighs. On collecting this, his first patient, Matt was surprised that he was given few details other than to deliver him to the Field Hospital in Kuwait City; and strangely for a Marine, he didn't have a personal weapon with him. 'Murph' and the Driver confirmed where they were headed and what route to take and they started the long drive. Matt in the back began to take down a few details in his notebook (There were no Field Medical Cards available at this time) so when they arrived in Kuwait City he could brief the staff at the Field Hospital about his patient. The US Marine seemed friendly enough and explained that he had a chest infection and was coughing up green phlegm, other than that he seemed to be perfectly fit and healthy. Matt explained that a lot of the coalition troops had chest infections due to the change in climate and the infernal sand storms, he also told the Marine that in a couple of days the infection would probably clear up. What Matt's patient seemed to be more concerned about was "Getting back with my buddies before they go over the berm (a built up earth embankment that signified the border between Saudi Arabia and Iraq) and into combat, do you think my chest infection will keep me out of combat?" Matt explained that would be up to the doctor who examined him in the hospital and for the rest of the journey they chatted about differences between the US and British Armies.

On arrival at the Field Hospital the ambulance backed up to the reception area and Matt opened the rear doors, as the US Marine stepped out of the ambulance he was set upon by two RMP's (Royal Military Policemen) who forced him onto the ground and clamped him in a set of steel handcuffs. Matt thought, 'That seems a bit excessive just for a chest infection'. As the Marine was frog marched away Matt asked the Sergeant in charge of reception, "What the fuck was that all about Sarge?" He replied, "Oh! Didn't you know; that US Marine soldier shot his Platoon Officer because he didn't want to do a guard duty?" During the four-hour trip to Kuwait, Matt's SA 80 was within arms length of a bloke who could have snapped his neck like a twig.

Sergeant Ritchie John RADC

During the four-week acclimatisation Exercise Ritchie and his team of 'Gob Doctors' worked in their CDC tent decontaminating simulated chemical casualties. They found working in the one hundred plus degrees heat of the Saudi desert unbearable and to compound the problem they had to wear full NBC (Nuclear, Biological, and Chemical) kit; this included suits with hoods, rubber gloves, and over-boots.

67

They also had to wear their respirators whilst working in the CDC. The CDC team used the gas proof drinking device on the mouthpieces of their respirators, when connected to their gas proof water bottles they were able to try and take on board as much fluid as possible. But it wasn't enough though and Ritchie found his team were sweating so heavily they were becoming severely dehydrated, it also became clear that once they had consumed the contents of their water bottles; there was no way of refilling them in a gassed area. A line of ambulances started to form a queue with more simulated casualties, as they had to wait for Ritchie and his CDC team to get the casualties through the decontamination process. After working for an hour they were all exhausted and they had only decontaminated three casualties.

Fifty meters away from the CDC was the Field Ambulance Reception where the Medics and Doctors waited to receive the first simulated casualties, they worked in a system called COLPRO (Collective Protection), which is a forced air flow bubble with air locks, where the staff working in the bubble technically, don't have to wear NBC suits and respirators but are advised to at least wear respirators just in case Ritchie and his team didn't do their job properly and the casualties entered COLPRO with chemical contamination still on their clothing and were off gassing. The bubble is made of a semi permeable material and is inflated by generators that purify the air and pump it into the bubble to inflate it and give it its sausage shape, with the air being forced into the bubble and escaping through the pores of the material. It stopped any chemicals getting inside where the medics worked. The bubble was housed inside a huge 18x24 tent.

If the Iraqis did go chemical, and there was a very real thought that they might because they had used them in the

Iran/Iraq War, then the Field Ambulances would be swamped and overloaded with real casualties and the likelihood was they'd be unable to cope. Staff Sergeant Bob Darkin orchestrated the running of the Field Ambulance Dressing Station and he noticed that because of the difficulties Ritchie and his team were having in the CDC; soldiers' lives would be at stake if they couldn't get them into the bubble and treated faster. Ritchie needed a lot more staff to enable him to get his job done. The CO (Commanding Officer) of 3 AFA arranged for twenty four Pioneer Corps soldiers to be permanently attached to Ritchie's CDC, they were all very fit and enthusiastic and they quickly adapted to their new role under Ritchie's guidance. They did the bulk of the manual work, which included lifting the casualties and cutting off their NBC suits whilst the RADC lads supervised what they were doing. The extra staffing worked wonders and casualties were getting into the bubble in record time throughout the rest of the Exercise.

Once the Exercise was completed the Pioneers Corps soldiers, with the army's usual idiocy, were moved to somewhere else and Ritchie was again left with just him and four 'Gob Doctors'.

Corporal Mick Killeen RAMC

The night the Allied Forces crossed the Iraq border Mick was being bounced around the back of his ambulance whilst reading an emotional letter from his daughter Victoria. In a similar fashion to all British Army soldiers, he tried to cry as quietly as possible so his other crewmembers wouldn't notice. Mick wasn't scared of the coming action that he might face, he just had a grim determination to get the damned thing over and done with and get back home in one

69

piece. An 18-foot high sand berm marked the border and the tarmac road they were travelling on ran through a gap at this border crossing point. Mick was distracted by the sound of gunfire and looked through the small window into the cab of the ambulance; a Yank soldier was firing a .50 calibre heavy machine gun at some poor bastard. The green tracer rounds that seemed to slowly arc their way towards its target fascinated Mick. He wondered how a bullet could appear to travel that slowly. The American soldiers he had seen the day before were wearing Ninja Turtle style bandanas and shouting, "We're gonna kill some bad asses" and "Kill, Kill, Kill." In comparison the British were walking around and saying, "Good luck mate, see you later."

5 GS Medical Regiment moved up to an assembly point and laagered up with some other British units, they were located just to the side of a tarmac road and it was still dark but their Union Jack flags easily identified them. A convoy of US Army vehicles was travelling along the road passing Mick's assembly point; a Hummer vehicle was escorting it with a soldier manning a .50 calibre heavy machine gun on the top of the lead vehicle. When he spotted the British vehicles and realised they were not Hummers, Dodges or Abram Tanks and were not flying the 'Good Old Stars and Stripes', he automatically assumed that Mick and his Oppo's were the enemy. He started firing into the British Assembly Point and Mick saw some of the tracer rounds hitting the ground near his ambulance. Two British Challenger tanks immediately charged out of the laager area dragging their scrim nets behind them and set off to educate the US soldier about the British Army's views of fire discipline. Luckily there were no casualties.

Captain Sharon Anthony QARANC

After the sand storm had ceased, everyone in 1 CS was dashing about before running towards a couple of 4 tonners, Sharon shouted to the Squadron OC who was a Major and Regular Army female doctor, "Hey! Don't leave me here on my own, where are you all going?" The snooty OC said, "We're all going to have a Regimental photograph taken before the war kicks off." "Hang on" said Sharon, "I'll go and get my beret and kit." The OC venomously replied, "Oh no! You won't be in the photo, this is for Regulars only, you and the other Territorial's are definitely not part of this unit. I stated at the start of this deployment that I didn't want any TA soldiers in my Squadron!"

Sharon went back to the Collecting Sections 12x12 tent and sat on her own; she felt very lonely and wanted to go home.

Lance Corporal Matt Fairclough RAMC

Juliet Troop Crew Members were only allowed to sleep in their ambulances when it was raining, at all other times they had to basher up outside the vehicle. One night, about two weeks after Matt and his Crew had arrived in Saudi, it was pissing down with rain and 'Paddy' was sleeping on the stretcher, 'Murph' was sleeping on the seats and Matt was trying to sleep on the floor of the ambulance. The following conversation started:

Paddy: "Matt, you know how the army works."

Matt: "Yeah."

Paddy: "Do you think we'll be going home soon?"

Matt: "No fucking way mate, not till the war is over, why?"

Paddy: "Well, I thought we'd only be out here for two weeks, you know, like our usual Summer Camps, and this would be to qualify us for our bounty money. I didn't think we'd have to do all this extra stuff."

Matt: "If the war doesn't go well we could be out here for over a year."

Paddy: "Oh shit…my wife is going to kill me!"

Sergeant Ritchie John RADC

During the pre-war Exercise phase 3 AFA moved up towards the Iraq border and were located just behind the fighting elements of 7 Armoured Brigade, every time Ritchie attended a unit O Group (A daily briefing headed by the Commanding Officer which the senior rank of all departments must attend) he sat with Staff Sergeant Bob Darkin and didn't listen to a word that was said. They might as well have been speaking Swahili for all the good it was doing Ritchie. The CO waffled on about where they were in relation to the FEBA (Forward Edge of the Battle Area), which units they were operating in support of and by what time all departments should be RTM (Ready To Move), British Officers cannot talk without using acronyms. All Ritchie heard at the daily briefings was, "Blah Blah Blah. Oh, and by the way gentlemen, please be aware of the fact that Blah Blah Blah." When he did listen, he didn't understand anything anyone was talking about, he then went back to the CDC to brief his own team. When the lads asked what was said at the O Group; Ritchie told them the only thing that he could remember, "Breakfast is at 0730 hours,

72

oh yes, and weapons must be cleaned beforehand." Ritchie knew about the technicalities of running a CDC, but as for his knowledge of how the Military system worked and man managing a team of soldiers, he was totally out of his depth.

Corporal Mick Killeen RAMC

Mick had dealt with a couple of minor casualties in the back of his ambulance when he realised that he didn't feel confident or competent in the job of 'medic'. He had to turn to Derek every time for medical treatment advice, as a highly qualified and experienced Paramedic in civilian life Derek should have been in the back and not sat in the front of the ambulance map reading and operating the radio. Mick was an experienced Radio Operator, excellent map-reader and unflappable JNCO. After just a quick lesson he also found the Magellan portable GPS equipment issued to all crew leaders very easy to use. In a copycat scenario to the British Army in the Second World War, when a civilian mechanic was conscripted and told, "Trained mechanic? Right you can be a cook," Mick and Derek had been put in the wrong jobs.

The RAMC during the Gulf War had filled every military appointment with about as much thought as the British Army of the 1940's did. According to Mick, Derek was exceptional at the medical caring side of their job and Mick was damn good at the map reading and communication's side of their life. Without consulting the officers at 5 GS Medical Regiment Headquarters, who would only have complicated matters, Mick and Derek swapped jobs.

Captain Sharon Anthony QARANC

All coalition forces were under strict instructions not to use their personal mobile phones to contact family and friends; each soldier was given a 20-minute phone card that could be used on the military satellite phones. In the Regimental Headquarters tent there were four chunky green satellite phones available for use.

Sharon tried to phone Mick when she was given her allotted 20 minute slot to use the phone; it wasn't as easy as using a telephone in the UK, at times satellites weren't available and connections could be bad. Sharon's connection problem was even more insurmountable; Mick was down the pub with their son Stephen. Mick had been glued to Sky TV since Sharon had left for the Gulf in the hope of seeing Sharon or getting some vital piece of information, anything to find out what was happening. Stephen had taken him down to the pub for a Sunday lunch just to try and take his mind of the forth-coming war. Sharon was upset she didn't get to hear Mick's voice but left a message for him, Mick and Stephen were gutted when they came back from the pub.

Lance Corporal Matt Fairclough RAMC

3 Para (3rd Battalion of the Parachute Regiment) was the main unit Matt and the rest of Juliet Troop were going to support in the initial advance into Iraq. The Paras QM (Quartermaster) issued all ambulance crewmembers with 100 rounds of ammunition each and at least a couple of different coloured smoke grenades. These were to be used for identification purposes when dealing with allied aircraft. The ambulances were laagered up with the rest of the Air Assault Brigade and were surrounded by a mass of vehicles which included stripped down Land Rovers that were

bristling with machine guns and 4 tonners full of either stores or heavily armed paratroopers.

Whilst with 5 GS Medical Regiment Matt and his Crew Members had been living on a diet of all in stew or the US Forces MRE's (Meals Ready to Eat), which the British Troops had re-designated, Meals Rejected by Ethiopians. But now they were attached to 3 Para and the night before they went over the border and into Iraq, the scoff consisted of chicken and chips. This was their first decent meal since arriving in Saudi Arabia and after scoffing the lot down Matt said to 'Murph' "Do you think they're fattening us up for the kill." 'Murph' just chuckled.

As the time to H hour ticked down the only things to occupy the mass of soldiers stuck in the middle of the desert was smoking, sleeping and smoking some more when they woke up. Matt had never smoked so many cigarettes in his entire life, during one of these Gold Medal winning smoke breaks, 'Murph' laid out the operating procedures for their personal part in the war. "Each crew will take it in turns to lead on a mission, as neither of the ambulances has any air conditioning both will be used for the treatment and movement of casualties. If we have to pick up more than one casualty they will be evenly distributed between both vehicles." Of their own ambulance 'Murph' stated, "I'll do all the map reading, radio work and decision making and leave you free to deal solely with the casualty, however, if you need any help or advice on anything clinical just give me a shout." Matt felt slightly daunted about what he may face when it all kicked off. With an Armoured Field Ambulance the tracked armoured ambulances would pick up the casualties from the RAP (Regimental Aid Post) on the FEBA (Forward Edge of the Battle Area) and take them back to the Field Ambulance DS (Dressing Station), from here the soft skinned ambulances would take the casualty back to the Field Hospital after they were stabilised. The Air Assault Brigade didn't have any armoured ambulances so the thin skinned ambulances would have to be used to cover all stages of the medical evacuation set up. Matt was daunted but he had asked for the job and they had trained him for it, so now he had to get on with it.

Sergeant Ritchie John RADC

The NBC experts visited 3 AFA from the MOD's NBC Training Centre at Winterbourne Gunner near Salisbury, they came to inspect the medics' NBC equipment and make sure their NBC SOP's (Standard Operating Procedures) were being adhered to. A worse case scenario had to be considered and every unit had to be ready to operate in a chemical environment before the coalition troops could advance into Iraq.

They checked out Ritchie's CDC and seemed quite happy with all his NBC equipment, where the department was located in relation to the rest of the Field Ambulance, and the scale of personnel in his Department (the Pioneer Corps soldiers hadn't been moved on at this stage). The inspecting NBC specialists also paid particular attention to the expiry dates on the filtration canisters on the COLPRO inflation units; contaminated air would be sucked through these to clean the air that would inflate the bubble where the surgeons would be inside and treating the casualties. The canisters were a couple of years past their sell by date and were therefore deemed to be, according to SSgt Bob Darkin, "Fucking useless", anyone working inside the bubble would obviously be at risk of chemical agent poisoning. The inspecting officers got past this minor problem, not by putting on new canisters; because none were available; he simply changed the expiry date on the canister with his permanent marker pen.

Corporal Mick Killeen RAMC

Mick and his crew co-workers were at Headquarters 7 Armoured Brigade when a scud missile exploded about ½ a kilometre from where they were parked. Yellow smoke was coming from the remnants of the missile as every Land Rover in the near vicinity was sounding their horns, one second on and one second off, which is one of the signs to warn soldiers of a chemical attack.

There was no panic from anyone, the NBC (Nuclear, Biological, and Chemical Warfare) Drills that every soldier had carried out thousands of times in training just kicked in. Close eyes, stop breathing, mask up in less than nine seconds, and then get into your full Noddy suit, boots and black 'Marigold' gloves. Then turn to the man nearest to you and use the 'Buddy, Buddy' system and check each others clothing and equipment too make sure everyone has a gas proof seal around their respirator. Everything seemed to work and all that incessant NBC training that every soldier in the British Army hated seemed to have paid off.

Mick was calm but his heart rate had increased significantly and he found his breathing was much laboured, was he suffering from Nerve Agent poisoning? Or was his body just reacting to the stress of the situation? He started to think to himself, 'Fuck! Why didn't I take those fucking NAPS tablets'! They all remained masked up for the next hour until the Brigade NBC Cell Controller issued orders for everyone to unmask, there was no chemical contamination.

Captain Sharon Anthony QARANC

1 CS held an NBC (Nuclear Biological and Chemical) Exercise which involved them all being masked up for 24 hours; it was done so they could get acclimatised to working in full NBC IPE (Individual Protection Equipment) in the event of the Iraqis using chemical weapons. The only thing the Exercise achieved was dehydrating everyone in the unit and making them all hypoglycaemic (low blood sugar); they couldn't get enough fluids and food inside themselves because they had to wear respirators (Gas Masks) all the time.

Sharon felt the time on the NBC Exercise would have been better spent on defining people's roles and setting up procedures. Pissing about in Noddy suits and respirators just to mess people about served no purpose what so ever. As well as being collared for general and menial duties during the Exercise, Sharon also treated patients for grit in their eyes, conjunctivitis, dehydration, hypoglycaemia, and minor cuts and bumps.

The satellite phones in RHQ were shut down for 24 hours and Sharon noticed US tanks and armoured vehicles were thundering past 1CS in the general direction of Iraq. It didn't take the brains of a General to work out that the coalition forces were about to move forward into Iraq.

Lance Corporal Matt Fairclough RAMC

Juliet Troop Sergeant summoned all his ambulance crews for an O Group (Orders Group) and told them that the latest order from on high was for everyone to start taking their NAPS (Nerve Agent Pre- treatment Set) tablets. One tablet is supposed to be taken every eight hours for seven days to help slow down the awful effects of nerve agent poisoning and allow a soldier time to inject himself with his Combo Pens which is an antidote to Nerve Agent poisoning. One hour after taking his first tablet Matt's jaw locked up and he was in considerable pain for two hours; thereafter every time the Troop Sergeant came round to check Matt had taken his NAPS tablet, Matt just pretended to swallow it and after the Sergeant had left he just spat it out. Matt went through this charade every eight hours.

Sergeant Ritchie John RADC

The NBC inspection team put a chemical agent simulant on the pretend casualties prior to Ritchie and his team decontaminating them, the simulant would show up in a blue haze under an ultra violet light and the team could show Ritchie and his lads whether or not they were doing the job properly. After several simulated casualties had been through the system; the NBC inspection team used their ultra violet torches to check the route the casualties had followed from Ritchie's CDC through to the COLPRO where the pretend casualties had their pretend medical treatment.

The dirty side of the CDC was covered in a blue haze under the beam of the torches and Ritchie and his team were covered from head to toe in the same glow. The clean side of the CDC and all the equipment in it was in pretty much the same state; the inspection team followed a trail of footprints across the sand to the Field Ambulance Reception area and into the COLPRO. The simulated contaminant was showing up everywhere, including in the airlocks on the COLPRO and even on the surgeons' hands after they had handled the incoming stretchers. Staff Sergeant Bob Darkin pointed out the obvious, "Fucking hell! If this was a real chemical agent all this kit would now be unusable, half the CDC team would be casualties themselves because they have cut their gloves and fingers whilst cutting off the casualty's NBC suits. Not only that, but we wouldn't have any surgeons because they would be involuntarily pissing and shitting themselves whilst having an epileptic fit on the floor of the COLPRO, this ain't going to fucking work!" The inspection team leader tried to reassure Ritchie and Bob when he said, "Ah well…I'm sure it will be alright on the night."

Corporal Mick Killeen RAMC

At the Ramallah Oil Terminal two Iraqi girls had stood on a landmine, one of the six-year-old pair of cousins had lost a leg because of the explosion. They had both been operated on and stabilised, Mick and his crew had been detailed to pick them up from the Field Hospital and transport them to the Kuwait border to another medical facility.

Both girls were clutching small teddy bears that the staff of the Field Hospital had given them; the hospital had a stack of them for just this type of scenario. After loading the girls in the back of the ambulance Mick was grabbed by one of the girl's father's, he was crying and started kissing Mick's hands saying, "Thank you, thank you so much, you have saved their lives, how can I ever repay you?"

Mick felt guilty for receiving such gratitude because he hadn't actually done anything, he was only picking them up and taking them somewhere else in his ambulance. Mick's conscience bothered him as he thought, 'Fuck me, this bloke is thanking us but if we hadn't been here in the first place, none of this might even have happened'.

Captain Sharon Anthony QARANC

At the 1 CS O Group (Orders Group) the Commanding Officer warned all his officers that their unit were about to move forward into Iraq, they were given the sequence vehicle packets were to move in, RV Points (Relevant Grid Referenced areas on a map), mined areas and a whole host of important information that Sharon would later have to brief her Section about. Although Sharon was nervous, her main thought was, 'lets just get this whole thing over and done with so we can go home.'

After the briefing she was given a brief half hour lesson on how to use the Magellan GPS equipment and then immediately forgot how to use it, Sharon and her driver just followed the vehicle in front for the rest of the war. All the vehicle packets were behind the MTO's (Motor Transport Officer) Land Rover anyway and he knew exactly where they were going.

All personal incoming and outgoing mail had been stopped for two weeks prior to crossing over the border into Iraq; this was to prevent anyone getting wind of exactly when the allies were going to start moving forward. Sharon had treated some casualties prior to the start of the Coalition advance and before loading them into an ambulance she gave them two or three letters to post when they had been received at a Base Hospital. Sharon was using her head and starting to break the rules. Everyone in the unit was sterilised of personal letters and documents just in case they were captured, at this stage Sharon had only received one letter from home, and it was from Mick. There was no way she was going to give up this precious piece of home; so after blacking out her home address and Mick's name, Sharon put it back in her combat jacket pocket. It started to look like she was going to make a habit of breaking the rules.

Lance Corporal Matt Fairclough RAMC

The first casualty of the war for 3 Para was assigned to Matt and 'Murph's' crew, they had only just gone over the berm and the fighting hadn't even started. The crew approached 3 Para's RAP as their casualty was being carried out of a 12 by 12 tent; he was a burly Para in his mid twenties and wobbled on the stretcher on his hands and knees as he was carried towards the ambulance by the sniggering RAP staff. The very unhappy paratrooper was wearing a green army T shirt, socks and boots and appeared to be wearing some kind of nappy, on closer inspection Matt realised the nappy was in fact a mass of damp Shell Dressings. Matt supervised the loading of the stretcher into the ambulance and was handed the casualty's Field Medical Treatment Card with all his details and treatment received up to that point.

Once they got underway the Paratrooper, still positioned on all fours, explained what had happened to him. He had been having a shit on a four seated thunder-box that was positioned over a DLT (Deep Latrine Trench), the trench was ready to be burnt but was still in use by soldiers in the unit. After finishing his post-shit cigarette and before pulling up his combat trousers, he parted his legs and dropped the lit fag into the mass of excreta in the trench below him. The methane built up from faeces over a couple of days is particularly potent and the poor sods cigarette butt (Pardon the Pun) ignited the gas and burnt his bollocks and arse. The flash burns were only superficial but because of

82

the tender area affected; the casualty couldn't even walk without causing severe pain.

On the three and a half hour journey to the Field Hospital Matt tried to make light of the situation with a bit of mild banter, all this whilst pouring water over the embarrassed blokes arse and nuts to relieve his pain. The paratrooper growled, "Don't take the piss, 'cos when I get better, I'll come fucking looking for you!"

Sergeant Ritchie John RADC

A vaccinations parade was held in one of the treatment bays of 3 AFA so the medics could be inoculated, Sergeant John Carter RAMC was one of the first to go through the parade, and he had every jab that was available; there wasn't any point in taking chances. He was given Whooping cough, anthrax, plague and a cocktail of other vaccines to protect him from any possible Biological agents that may be used against the coalition forces. Unfortunately he had a systemic reaction to the injections and became unconscious for two days, his medic comrades bedded him down in his own accommodation tent in the hope that he would come round and be able to carry on with the war when it started.

At this time Ritchie had started taking PT parades for 3 AFA to keep the medics physically fit whilst they were stuck out in the middle of the desert, Bob Darkin was just checking up on John Carter's condition when Ritchie came into the accommodation tent, he was corralling all soldiers not on essential duties to take them for a run around the unit location. Aware of most soldiers' attempts to get out of any PT Parades Ritchie asked Bob, "Is he coming to the Gym this morning?" Bob laconically said, "No, he still unconscious, I think he's at death door mate." Ritchie raised his eyebrows, tutted and said, "Oh, alright then, if he comes round you can tell him he's excused this session."

Bearing in mind Sergeant John Carter's condition, Ritchie and Bob Darkin decided to question the MO (Medical Officer) about what vaccines they had to receive when it was their turn to be inoculated, "Out of all the diseases we could possibly get, which one is the worst?" The MO told the pair of them that the only one that was probably impossible to cure was plague, they both said, "Ok, we'll have that one, but none of the others."

Corporal Mick Killeen RAMC

The sand and dust storms had become so intense at times it was difficult for soldiers to work without an Arab style shemag to cover their heads and faces. The British Army didn't issue shemag's or any other similar textile for soldiers to protect themselves from the elements, but Mick noticed soldiers from other units had obviously served in the first Gulf War and had bought shemag's with them. He remembered he had a scarf at home that he used to wear when riding his motorbike to work; it was identical to what everyone else was wearing as a shemag.

Mick wrote home to Jean and asked her to send it out to him and it arrived about three weeks later, Jean had washed the scarf prior to sending it out and it smelled of Jean's usual fabric softener. The scarf arrived just as the sand storm season came to and end and Mick no longer needed it, but it still came in handy. Mick kept it in a plastic bag to retain its fragrant smell, and whenever he felt a bit down in the dumps he would take it out for a comforting snuffle. It was a tangible reminder of home.

Captain Sharon Anthony QARANC

Once over the border and into Iraq Sharon's driver Dave, the CMT 1 Lance Corporal, commented on the young Iraqi children waving at them, "Ah, isn't this great, look how pleased they are to see us." Later on Dave was mortified when he saw some Iraqi teenagers sticking two fingers up at them. Sharon told him "Think yourself lucky, if you were in Hull they would be chucking bricks at you."

Lance Corporal Matt Fairclough RAMC

Most of the ambulance crews met up at some time or other during the tour in Iraq, Matt met up with a crew who were all from his Hull TA unit. The Crew Commander was a female Lance Corporal CMT 1 called Mel, in Civvie Street she was a qualified Paramedic, the Lance Corporal Medic in the back was her fiancé and he was also a CMT 1 and whilst not serving in Iraq was a civilian fire fighter. The Driver of the ambulance was an RAMC Sergeant from Grimsby called 'Snowey' who was and still is the most inoffensive man you could meet anywhere in the world. In fact when he was a Corporal on Exercise back in the UK the other NCOs were always taking the piss because he kept apologising to Privates for giving them orders.

Whilst on Exercise in the UK with 250 Field Ambulance, Corporal Alan Scarborough, who was an ex Regular Army REME Vehicle Mechanic, tried to train 'Snowey' in the art of being more aggressive, they did some role play whilst sitting in the back of the REME wagon. Alan instructed 'Snowey' to come up behind him and tell him to "Get out of my fucking chair you bastard!" Snowey duly walked up behind Alan and repeated the lines given to him to read out

"Get out of my chair you swine!" Alan Scarborough jumped out of the chair and screamed in Snowey's face, "WHO THE FUCKING HELL DO YOU THINK YOU ARE TALKING TO!!!!! Snowey automatically reverted to type and said, "I'm so sorry mate, I thought we had started on the lesson." Alan carried on with the lessons over the rest of the weekend but it came to no avail, 'Snowey' was just a nice guy.

During the tour of Iraq 'Snowey's' fellow Crew members were getting very pissed off with him because of his annoying habit of constantly whipping his tea in a china cup with a metal spoon. Every time they had a brew all you could hear within earshot of their ambulance was CHING CHING CHING CHING CHING, and it was driving them crazy. As 'Snowey' was a Sergeant, his Crewmembers felt it would be undisciplined of them to complain about a SNCOs habits, so they whinged about it to Matt.

At 2230 hours whilst the Crews were trying to get some shuteye, 'Snowey' decided to make a cup of tea in his favourite china mug and was making the usual racket. Matt was awoken by the noise and shouted. "SNOWEY! IF YOU DON'T STOP MAKING THAT NOISE I'M GOING TO SHOVE THAT SPOON UP YOUR FUCKING ARSE!" Snowey quietly shouted "Sorry."

Corporal Alan Scarborough was right; you can't make a Crouching Tiger out of a Cuddly Kitten.

Sergeant Ritchie John RADC

Sergeant Olywoko was a Black Bandsman who was attached to 3 AFA as a stretcher-bearer; the piss takers in the unit called him the 'Grim Reaper' and without doubt he was the most depressing soldier Ritchie had ever met. One morning when Ritchie was having a shave standing at the unit water bowser; Sergeant Olywoka approached him with a towel round his neck and washing and shaving kit under his arm, as he set up his kit ready to start shaving he opened a conversation with Ritchie.

Sergeant Olywoko: "Good morning Ritchie my old friend, I don't think it will be long now."

Ritchie: "Won't be long before what?"

Sergeant Olywoko: "I think the Iraqi Army will descend upon us soon?"

Ritchie: "What?"

Sergeant Olywoko: "Will today be the day the gods of war are unleashed upon us and we all are left to our fate?"

Ritchie: "Fuck knows mate, I'm off to breakfast, see you later."

It was no different the following day, in fact Sergeant Olywoko seemed to deliberately time his ablutions so he could stand and talk to Ritchie.

Sergeant Olywoko: "Good morning Ritchie, Do you think the Iraqi's will try to gas us today before they send their tanks to crush us into the sands of the desert?"

Ritchie: "Bloody hell mate, you're a real bundle of laughs in the morning, what on earth makes you think I am privy to the tactics of the Iraqi Republican Guard, I don't even know what clothes to put on in the morning!"

Ritchie had a word with Bob Darkin, "Fuck me Bob; I know I can moan a bit but this guy takes the biscuit." Every morning Ritchie could be seen ducking behind the nearest tent to avoid having to talk to Sergeant Olywoko.

Corporal Mick Killeen RAMC

A lot of the coalition troops suffered from severe bouts of diarrhoea and vomiting whilst deployed to Iraq, Mick started to believe they had all been exposed to some form of biological agent. He went down with it himself and ended up being admitted to 34 Field Hospital for three days to receive treatment. He felt well enough to return to duty after 24 hours but patients could not leave until given the green light from the attending doctor. It was very busy in the tented hospital and every time Mick's doctor came to see him his bleeper went off as he was paged for yet another emergency.

The ward also included Iraqi POW's who had heard from other prisoners in their POW camps that if you feigned an illness you would end up in a bed with clean sheets, decent food and be tended to by large breasted porn stars and prostitutes who had to subject to their every whim. British Army nurses took a totally different view of their job description, so did the British Soldiers who were detailed to guard each POW who had been admitted to the hospital. The POW in the bed next to Mick started groping a nurse's crotch and breasts as she took his temperature, she jumped back and remonstrated him as the attending guard sprang into action and started rifle butting the POW in the face. Mick could see the POW was confused, he couldn't understand what he had done wrong, he believed that all Western women were like those he saw in his porno

88

magazines. At least one Iraqi prisoner had learned a painful and valuable lesson that he could take back to his mates in the POW camp.

Captain Sharon Anthony QARANC

Sharon could see palls of smoke in the distance and thought 'Shit, what are we heading into', they were on a tarmac road that would take them into Basra and who ever was in that area, they were taking a hell of a pasting. 1 CS were pulled over to the side of the road and told to wait there for an hour, a load of Yank Hummers that were armed to the teeth drove past them and headed to the battle area. Sharon and her unit were then moved on to a minor side road that led to a small town where they waited in their vehicles for hour after hour. As it got towards evening and the light started to fade, Sharon could see flashes of explosions from the artillery shells flying towards targets in and around Basra. Within the hour all the Yank Hummers she had seen earlier were screaming down the main road again, but this time they were heading back towards Kuwait. A thought popped into Sharon's head, 'Bloody hell, don't leave us here on our own!'

By the time darkness had descended on the desert Sharon started to get anxious, sitting around and waiting in their vehicles during the fog of war was bad enough but being in the dark made it a lot worse. Someone appeared out of the darkness at the passenger side window of her Land Rover and made Sharon jump out of her skin, "Bloody hell you twat, at least you could warn us you are approaching." It was getting really cold, so Sharon got into her sleeping bag to try and warm up a bit as she just sat there waiting. An unidentified low flying aircraft flew over their location and someone started shouting "GAS, GAS, GAS" so Sharon had to get out of her nice warm sleeping bag and get into full IPE after masking up. They remained like that for an hour before someone came round and told them they could all unmask and get out of their NBC Noddy Suits because it was a false alarm. Sharon took her respirator off but stayed in the Noddy Suit as it kept her warm. She just sat there and watched the Royal Artillery's very expensive firework display that was being put on in Basra.

Lance Corporal Matt Fairclough RAMC

The lads in Matt's crew spent a lot of time picking up casualties from the RAP (Regimental Aid Post) at 3 Para but not all of them were battle injuries. On this particular shout it was a TA paratrooper seconded from 4 Para to 3 Para, he was a burly but very friendly bloke who in civilian life worked in a bakery. He had gone over on his ankle and had probably just sprained it but the RMO was sending him for an x-ray at the nearest Field Hospital to make sure of his diagnosis. The tough paratrooper could walk but limped somewhat over to the ambulance carrying his SA80 rifle and climbed in the back with a little bit of help from 'Murph'. Matt picked up the casualty's webbing and threw it in the back of the ambulance, he them went back for the Para's Bergen, which was at the side of the RAP tent. As he attempted to lift the large item of equipment Matt grunted and felt the muscles in his back strain at the Bergen's very heavy weight, Matt leaned backwards and pulled the Para's equipment along the ground before struggling to get it in the back of the ambulance. The only comment he could make was, "Fucking hell mate, how do you get that fucking thing on your back."

After having his ankle x-rayed, the hospital confirmed the paratrooper had a severely fractured ankle.

Sergeant Ritchie John RADC

Morale within 3 AFA remained reasonably high even though they had moved location over a dozen times, and it didn't seem likely that the war was going to start in the near future, at least Ritchie didn't think anyone had mentioned it at any of the O Groups he attended. The rumours varied from, "The Yanks are waiting till the end of the month" to "Each side is too scared to start the fighting." When Ritchie's team erected their tent for the first time it was like watching the Keystone Cops being commanded by Stan Laurel. The team bumped into each other and accidently hit a soldier next to them on the head with tent poles whilst tripping over kit left lying on the ground. But four weeks later they had gelled into a team, everyone knew what they had to do when setting up the CDC and taking it down again when the unit was bugged out. They even managed to do it quietly at night with the same degree of competence, noise travels further at night and Staff Sergeant Bob Darkin was adamant that tent poles should not be clanged together and voices must be kept to a minimum. By the end of the Exercise the lads had moved so many times that they could set up their section and be ready to receive casualties within twenty minutes of arriving in the new location. When they moved out again they also packed everything on the vehicle neatly and in a logical order, even the heavy tents were packed away in their valises because Bob Darkin was pedantic about it being done properly.

At 0330 hours in the morning of 16th January; Ritchie was sound asleep in his doss bag and dreaming of German beer and sexy women when he was given a rude awakening.

When the time came Ritchie was expecting an earth-shattering announcement but instead, a wimpy clerk put his head through the tent flap and said, "Put on your helmets and full combats, the war has started."

Corporal Mick Killeen RAMC

During the Gulf War the US Forces carried on with the tradition from World War Two of throwing sweets and chocolate bars to the local children. "Got any gum, chum" was the call from children in England during the 1940's; the Iraqi kids didn't have a catchphrase but were equally as grateful for any sweets that were thrown to them. The British Army put out strict orders to all of its soldiers; they were not to give any confectionary to the local children. As a result of what the US Forces were doing; children were now running out in front of convoys to stop them in an attempt to get something to eat.

The Iraqi children took umbrage to the fact that the tight fisted Brits were not as generous as the Yanks; some British ambulances had large rocks thrown at their windscreens causing severe facial injuries to the Drivers and Crew Commanders. Mick attended a briefing given by his OC (Officer Commanding) who instructed them, "If you are attacked by children with bricks you must return fire and shoot to kill!" One of the TA lads said, "Can you just repeat that sir, you did say we were to shoot to kill." The OC confirmed his orders. Mick thought 'Fucking hell, that's a bit heavy'.

The next time Mick was out on a detail his team were transporting a casualty to a Field Hospital, some Iraqi 8 year old children started throwing rocks at Mick and his ambulance and obstructed their journey. Mick told the Driver to pull over. The casualty in the back of the rear ambulance started to get stressed out with the sound of rocks bouncing off the side of the ambulance. The children kept advancing on the two ambulances throwing more and more rocks, Mick wasn't sure what to do but he certainly wasn't going to 'shoot to kill' at an 8 year old petulant youngster. He cocked his SA 80 rifle and fired two shots into the air, the mischievous little sods bomb-burst in different directions allowing Mick and his crew to continue with their journey. Mick proudly says, "They were the only shots fired by Corporal Mick Killeen RAMC on Operation Telic 1."

Mick ignored the OC's policies on this subject and went back to throwing sweets at the kids; it seemed a lot less hassle.

Captain Sharon Anthony QARANC

In the early hours of the next morning 1 CS moved back onto the main road heading into Basra and turned off it again onto another main road, their progress was painfully slow and fragmentary. They spent another twenty-four hours at the side of the road unwittingly waiting, waiting, and waiting. Sharon tried to join in with group conversations as they all stood around the section vehicles laughing and joking, but as she walked up to the crowds of soldiers the conversation would die down and become very stilted. Sharon was the only TA soldier and officer in the Section she was there to command; and because they were all Regular Army there was a certain amount of distrust and disdain towards her. Football was eventually the key icebreaker between Sharon and her Section, when the lads found out she was an avid fan of Sky's Soccer AM television programme, and that she could hold an in depth

93

conversation on all aspects of the presenters and its comedy routines, she became one of the lads.

Whilst waiting at the side of the road they had plenty of time to make brews and heat up their ration packs, Sharon can vividly remember what she ate because the unit was given the same menu every day for four weeks (24-hour Ration Pack Menu G). Beef and tomato soup was the starter followed by beef spread and biscuits. For the main course it was meatballs and pasta followed by a chocolate pudding.

Iraqi refugees walked past the 1 CS vehicles and medics as they waited at the side of the road and some made a point of shaking the medics' hands and thanking them profusely. The medics gave the shabby looking civilians some of their water and rations, they had to be careful though as they only carried enough water and rations to sustain them for four days, and no guarantee of when they would get the next re-supply from the Quartermaster.

One of the refugees was pushing a moped with a large box strapped on the back; he was struggling as he pushed it along the road because it had two flat tyres. Taffy and another lad from Sharon's Section stepped forward and gave the Iraqi a hand with his unwieldy burden but he seemed to be wary and nervous of the British soldiers. A British Army Warrior AFV (Armoured Fighting Vehicle) came flying down the road from the direction the refugees had been walking; the guy pushing the moped threw it down on the floor and started running. Another Iraqi who had come from behind some bushes to help him also spotted the Warrior and decided to join his mate in his bid for freedom. The infantry debussed from their AFV and jumped on the two Iraqis and pinned them down on the ground, their Section Commander took out some weapons that were hidden in the box on the back of the moped. He had been looking for the pair of them and spotted the medics giving them a helping hand and pounced before they could disappear. From that point onwards Sharon became less trusting of the Iraqi people.

Lance Corporal Matt Fairclough RAMC

All the 5 GS Medical Regiment ambulance crews that were operating in support of 3 Para had to adopt the Airborne Forces rules when they were in their locations and on one particular night they were told that everyone had to be on a hard routine. This entailed no smoking or cooking of any food in the location; and it also meant that light and noise discipline was to be rigidly kept to a minimum, headlights on the ambulances were not to be switched on under any circumstances.

Two hundred meters from where Matt's ambulance was co-located with 3 Para was a burning oil wellhead that Saddam Hussein's retreating troops had deliberately sabotaged. The roaring sound was as equally deafening as the heat was intense; everything was lit up for miles around making it easy for Matt not to use his headlights and it also covered up any noise that he and ten thousand troops might make. As the black acrid smoke from the wellhead rose into the night sky; Matt noticed black greasy droplets falling from above and landing on his arms.

Sergeant Ritchie John RADC

Half an hour after the war had officially been started, 3 AFA's radio operators heard a report on the network that a Scud B missile was heading towards their location, and as a result of this Ritchie could hear someone shouting, "GAS,

GAS, GAS!" This was the first threat of a chemical attack since they had arrived in Saudi Arabia and Ritchie describes the moment in his war diary, "At this juncture, in a manner of speaking, I shat myself." At 0400 hours when you are tired, but suddenly woken up and adrenalin starts pumping round the body, it can be hard to keep your thoughts in a rational state. But that was exactly what everyone did, Ritchie's war diary goes on, "The lads were worried, they were silent but responded to every command without thinking. I had to remain calm and reassure them. It was bloody hard." The reality of the situation was hitting home for Ritchie.

Corporal Mick Killeen RAMC

Some military ambulances were occasionally used during the war to treat and transport civilian casualties; Mick's crew had a woman bought to them by her family and she had 30% burns to her body and arms. A gaggle of wailing women and men carried her into the ambulance and placed her on the stretcher, none of the medics could understand a word of what they were saying as they were babbling in their native Iraqi tongue. Strangely, the Iraqi women outside the ambulance were slapping the bottom of the casualty's feet that were hanging over the end of the stretcher. Derek and the other medic were assessing her burns and the woman, who was conscious and in a great deal of pain, pulled back some of her clothing on her chest to show them how bad her burns were.

Mick was sitting in the front of the ambulance giving a Sitrep (Situation Report) on the radio and working out the route they were going to take to get the poor woman to the nearest medical facility. All of a sudden the ambulance started violently rocking from side to side as an almighty punch up erupted in the back, one of the male relatives was offended by the fact that the casualty had exposed herself to these infidels and had started to punch her in the face. Derek and the other medic were equally offended by his appalling actions and forcefully ejected him and his relatives out the back of the ambulance. After bundling them all out of the vehicle both crews and ambulances sped off to get the casualty further medical treatment.

Captain Sharon Anthony QARANC

Because of the Sections apathy towards her, Sharon found company and solace from the Padre attached to 1 CS Medical Regiment and the SDG's (Scots Dragoon Guards). Captain Ian Richardson was a down to earth Scottish Roman Catholic Priest who had a loud and dirty laugh that could be heard from a mile away, he also came out with some of the dirtiest jokes Sharon had ever heard. Ian treated Sharon exactly like the soldiers back in 250 treated her, he abused, insulted, and remorselessly took the piss out of everyone he met and Sharon was no exception. The SDG soldiers respected him as a man and not because of his rank, religion, or position, having said that he wasn't a paragon of virtue because he had a bad temper. On opening a parcel he had received from the UK he took out yet another set of rosary beads and was heard to shout, "Not more fucking rosary beads, why doesn't somebody send me some fucking food!" He wasn't a morning person either and as he got tangled up in his mosquito net getting out of his camp bed in the morning, cries of "Jesus H fucking Christ" could be heard around the location and someone would call out "The Padres up." His was the only vehicle, that Sharon knew of, that carried any smuggled alcohol (Sacramental Wine, whiskey and other spirits) in the coalition Forces. Everyone in the unit was warned that Kuwait and Iraq were 'Dry States' and therefore the entire deployment would be a 'Dry Exercise', on being told this Ian exclaimed "Dry Exercise…my arse!"

Captain Ian Richardson RAChD (Royal Army Chaplain Department) kept Sharon from getting depressed and going insane.

Lance Corporal Matt Fairclough RAMC

Matt's dad Harry had sent out magazines, food stuff and some ski goggles that he had asked for, the sand storms made it impossible to see anything without some sort of eye protection. Apart from his desire for Haribo fruit gums he also wanted some curry powder that he could mix in with his compo rations to make them more appetizing. Harry also sent him some mild porno magazines like Loaded and Penthouse. When Harry purchased the magazines from the NAAFI shop at Leconfield he explained to the young girl behind the counter, "They're for my son who is serving out in Iraq." She replied, "Yeah! I'm sure they are… you old perv!"

Matt took out a large poster of three semi naked women from the centre of the Loaded magazine; the women were holding an oversized and condensation-covered bottle of Becks lager. He stuck the poster on the inside roof of his ambulance above where the stretcher was positioned, every British and American casualty he carried seemed to be distracted from their pain or discomfort during the journey to hospital.

Sergeant Ritchie John RADC

One of Ritchie's CDC team was a strange lad called Lance Corporal Steve Mercer RADC; he liked to walk out into the desert and get away from the unit location to seek out and capture any wildlife that was out there. He made up a menagerie of desert creatures using a wooden ammunition crate he had found, the wooden structure imprisoned two large scorpions, a couple of lizards and a snake, he put sand, rocks and some plastic toys in the box so the occupants of his 'farm' felt at home and didn't get bored. Ritchie was indifferent about the 'farm' but was curious about whether or not the snake was poisonous.

Corporal Mick Killeen RAMC

After delivering more casualties to 34 Field Hospital, Mick's crew were preparing to return to their own unit. An Officer and an Infantry soldier who was wearing full Battle Order equipment including ammunition, SA 80 and bayonet approached them. The Officer ordered, "This chap has been discharged from 34 Field Hospital as fit and needs to get back to his Regiment, as you will be passing his unit's location, you can drop him off on your way!" Derek replied, "No we can't Sir. We are travelling in an ambulance and under the Rules of the Geneva Convention we cannot be used as a Troop Carrier. I am afraid, Sir, you will have to make other arrangements to get this soldier back to his unit." If RAMC soldiers are caught exploiting the sacrosanct instructions of the Geneva Convention, they forfeit all the rights and protection that are afforded to them as Red Cross bearers.

The Officer started to lose his rag and told Derek that he would do as he was "Bloody well told," but Derek wasn't prepared to do as he was "Bloody well told." Again he refused to comply with the order because he knew exactly what the repercussions would be for all ambulance crews if they were caught. The usual threats were issued but Derek would not be moved on the subject, he was not going to transport a fit, fighting soldier up to the front line under the cover of the Red Cross. Mick openly says, "If the Officer had asked me, I would have taken the guy back to his unit, purely and simply because it wouldn't even have occurred to me I was doing something wrong. But Derek was an experienced medic and knew all the rules." The officer would no doubt have been indignantly outraged if the Iraqi Army were caught doing such a 'dastardly deed', but as it was 'Our Side' he deemed it to be acceptable. The Officer went away to arrange some alternative transport for his stranded soldier.

Captain Sharon Anthony QARANC

Trip flares were set up around the Section every time they parked up at night just in case the Iraqi forces tried a night attack; Sharon's Section Sergeant also allotted everyone defensive Stand To positions for the same reason. When all arcs of fire had been covered around their location it left no one to man the treatment bay if they had any casualties, Sharon told her Sergeant that she would require one other person beside herself to man the treatment bay if they were attacked. He didn't like the fact that his Stand To orders were being countermanded by a TA female officer but he backed down as Sharon would not be moved on the subject. Since taking over the Section Sharon had noticed her Sergeant had been objectionable, he never cooked his own food and always expected one of the Privates from the

Section to do it for him. She also noticed some of the medical boxes were in a mess and told him to get them sorted out, he didn't bother, and when Sharon took him to task he blamed one of the Privates. This was the last straw for Sharon and she took him to one side and gave him the headlines, "You need to sort yourself out because you treat your lads like dirt, if you don't give them any respect, they won't respect you!" The Sergeant was so miffed at this dressing down he went and complained to the Dressing Station Staff Sergeant who came up to Sharon and patted her on the back. It seemed the Sergeant wasn't a popular SNCO; the bollocking Sharon gave him didn't improve his attitude either.

Lance Corporal Matt Fairclough RAMC

'Murph' 'Paddy' and Matt were standing round the bonnet of their ambulance and checking their location on the map with the help of the Magellan Sat Nav equipment, just as they had pinpointed their location the three of them were startled by an explosion followed by the screams of people in pain. About 100 meters up the road was an old fuel tanker lying on its side, it had been there for some time and was empty of fuel, but that didn't stop an Iraqi family trying to get the last possible dregs of petrol from it. It must have been a vapour hazard that had caused the explosion because the vehicle failed to burn after the explosion; it was uncertain what caused the vapour to ignite.

Matt says, "Murph was absolutely brilliant, he and I grabbed the Crash Bags and headed towards where the screams were coming from, there were three casualties, a middle aged mother and father and their young daughter." The girl had partial burns to her hands and the front of her legs and the father had full thickness burns to his arm, hand, and chest.

101

The mother also had full thickness burns to her face and upper chest, as they approached the casualties 'Murph' shouted at Matt, "Look after her, and I will deal with the other two!" The poor woman was unconscious but Matt could hear she was having difficulty in breathing; the smell of burnt human flesh and hair was nauseating. Although Matt didn't know it at the time, the casualty had more than likely inhaled super heated gases from the explosion which would have caused a swelling effect in her throat, it wouldn't be long before the swelling would close the larynx and she would asphyxiate. In scenarios like this it is essential to insert an ET Tube (Endotracheal Tube) in the casualty's mouth and down into the larynx to maintain a clear passage of air to the lungs so the casualty can breathe.

To insert an ET tube medics have to use an instrument called a laryngoscope, which has a handle the size of a small torch, and a folding banana shaped appendage with a small light at the tip. After switching on the light; the tip of the appendage is pushed into the casualty's mouth on the right side of the tongue, which pushes the tongue to the left side of the mouth, the tip should be advanced until the medic can see the epiglottis and then he pulls back on the handle and lifts the laryngoscope in an up and away from the prone casualty direction. An ET tube, which should have already been smothered in KY Jelly, is inserted down the throat and guided by the laryngoscope into the larynx, which is the upper of the two apertures as you look down the throat and leads down to the lungs. The lower aperture leads down to the stomach and if the tube goes in there it can lead to gastric inflation, which, as the casualty is in a prone position, can lead to gastric fluids seeping into the lungs. When the ET Tube is in the correct position a small balloon surrounding the base of it is inflated using a syringe full of air, this will form a good seal, and helps secure the tube in place. An ammby bag is a soft rugby ball shaped rubber bladder that is secured on the end of the tube and as it is squeezed air is forced into the casualty's lungs and it will re-inflate itself when the medics grip is released ready for the next breath.

Matt can't remember the full details of the procedure that he followed but several minutes later 'Murph' appeared along side him and said, "What the fuck have you done? Have you done this procedure before?" Matt replied, "Only on a training aid." 'Murph' took his stethoscope from around his neck and listened to the casualty's lungs before looking up at Matt and saying, "Fucking well done mate, good job!" It was at this point that Matt noticed his hands were trembling and he was sweating even more than he usually did in the mid day heat.

The casualties' wounds were dressed with shell dressings and burns bags (If you stop air getting to a burn it decreases a casualties pain significantly) and they were loaded into the ambulance and rushed to a Field Hospital about thirty minutes drive away.

Sergeant Ritchie John RADC

Ritchie enjoyed the food served up in the Field Ambulance cookhouse tent, but this was when they deployed on the four-week acclimatization Exercise, the food was varied and there seemed to be plenty of fresh rations. But since 3 AFA had gone on a war footing the food the chef's were serving up was mainly Compo Rations, Compo is high calorie tinned food that is quite bland, and if eaten for a long period can cause constipation.

The lads started to complain that every meal seemed to taste of a curried chicken flavour, when the ration stores Sergeant was summoned to find out why there wasn't any variation in the menus he broke down and cried. "I'm really sorry, when I picked up the rations for 3 AFA I didn't think about getting different menu ration packs, I've bought along one months supply of Ration Pack Menu A which is chicken curry."

The chefs did the best they could with what they had to work with and managed to serve up:

1. Curried chicken risotto.
2. Curried roast chicken.
3. Curried chicken stew.
4. Curried chicken pie.

Ritchie John is infamous for his love of a good 'Ruby Murray', but even he thought this was kicking the arse out of it.

Corporal Mick Killeen RAMC

5 GS Medical Regiment were going home, there was a rumour that they were going back to train for a deployment out to Bosnia. Everyone was excited about going home to be with their family and friends again, it had been a long and tough four-month tour, especially for the TA lads from Hull. For most of them it was their first operational deployment. Unfortunately they were given some bad news; all TA soldiers were staying out in Iraq with 1 CS Medical Regiment who were taking over the operational duties of 5 GS Medical Regiment. Naturally the TA lads were angry at being deserted by their own Regiment and didn't want to be absorbed into the new unit, they weren't the only ones who were angry, the Regular Army soldiers from 5 GS Medical Regiment felt ashamed of the way their TA oppo's were being treated. Some of them openly expressed their

104

sympathy and embarrassment at having to leave them behind.

Complaining about it wouldn't achieve anything, they just had to get on with it and wait their turn to go home. Mick was put with a new crew as 1 CS Medical Regiment shuffled everyone around to suit their requirements and generally piss everyone about. Mick was put with Corporal Mick Pallister who was to be the Medic, and the Driver was another TA soldier from Castleford called Bluey.

Captain Sharon Anthony QARANC

I CS was eventually co-located with the Brigade Headquarters at an abandoned Iraqi Air force airfield, units were not allowed to set up in the concrete hangars for fear of booby traps that the retreating Iraqi forces may have set. They also couldn't use the sand areas in case they were mined and the same problem meant they couldn't fill their sandbags. Everyone had to set up on the concrete hard standing, Sharon and most of the Medics were up and running within 10 minutes of being allocated an area from which to operate, the Brigade CP (Command Post) staff were still faffing around two hours later. After the Royal Engineers had swept and cleared the hangars for any possible dangerous explosive devices, then, and only then, could units move in and occupy the hangars.

1st Battalion of the Irish Guards had been moved back from the front line and were sited next to I CS's location and they set up security the other side of some sand dunes near Sharon's Section. Shots had been heard and there were reports of a sniper in the area resulting in the Irish Guards Squads running back over the sand dunes for cover. A young lad who hadn't applied the safety catch on his SA 80 rifle tripped and fell over, he was behind the rest of his squad and squeezed the trigger of his weapon as he fell and loosed off a round. The bullet hit his mate in the back of the thigh.

Sharon and Craig (The Scots Dragoon Guards Doctor) jumped into a Land Rover ambulance that was driven by Sharon's Section Sergeant and headed over to where the incident had happened. The casualty had a large flesh wound with no bony injury, the entry wound at the back and exit wound at the front of the thigh were obvious to Sharon, and she also noticed he had a lot of muscle loss due to the injury. The casualty didn't seem upset and appeared quite happy that he was now going back home to the UK. The Irish Guards RMA (Regimental Medical Assistant) Sergeant was really good and was efficiently dealing with him by the time Craig, Sharon and her Sergeant had arrived in the ambulance; he had applied a tourniquet and was about to administer a morphine autoject into casualty's' uninjured leg. Sharon's Section Sergeant took it off the RMA so he could do it himself but was holding it upside down and was about to fire it into his own thumb. The RMA Sergeant saw he was doing it wrong and took it back off him and administered it properly. Because of the sniper risk a temporary cover was put over the wound and they shifted the casualty on a stretcher into Sharon's Section Tent. Once inside the tent it was just like working through any ordinary working medical emergency in any medical practice within the UK. The RMA Sergeant completed dressing the wound and Sharon put together a Hartman's bottle and giving set whilst Craig put a cannula into his vein. When the life saving fluids were flowing into the casualty they gave him a full body check and monitored his blood pressure, pulse and respiration, the 19 year old casualty was later evacuated by Land Rover ambulance.

Lance Corporal Matt Fairclough RAMC

Matt and his crew were parked up in a 3 Para location at night on immediate standby; they were trying to get some shuteye whilst remaining fully clothed and ready to move at a minutes notice. Since crossing the border into Iraq there had been a constant barrage of NBC attack warnings and now someone else had heard yet another unidentified low flying aircraft overhead and started shouting "GAS! GAS! GAS!" Matt was sleeping in the passenger seat in the front of the ambulance and on hearing the alarm he raised his head off the side window and peered outside. The Paras were strolling around with their 'Airborne Wings of Steel' on the upper right shoulders of their uniforms; obviously assuming that the blue and white airborne badge rendered them impervious to any chemical agents. Either that or they just couldn't be arsed to go through the rigmarole of getting into full IPE (Individual Protection Equipment) again.

As the Paras weren't bothering to get into their NBC kit and were clearly not rolling around on the floor and gasping for breath; Matt thought, 'Fuck it, if they aren't going to bother then neither will I' and he went back to sleep. An hour later Matt was woken up by a Para tapping on his ambulance window, Matt showed his face to the Para and said, "What?" The Para sarcastically replied, "You can take your gas mask off now."

Sergeant Ritchie John RADC

Ritchie was bluffing his way through the war; he had so far just about managed to keep his head above water in a sea of military idiom he just didn't understand. It was about to get a whole lot worse for him.

One night Major Pilchard RADC came into the CDC tent and told Ritchie it was his turn to do watch-keeper in the CP (Command Post). Ritchie asked, "What is a CP and how do I watch-keep?" There were many units co-located with 3 AFA, including a Brigade Headquarters, just on the Saudi Arabian side of the border with Iraq. This CP was set up to co-ordinate all information coming into the units in that area, Ritchie was driven the short distance to the CP in a Land Rover. Even though it was night-time he could see communication aerials sticking though the camouflage net covering the Land Rover, the Land Rover also had a tent attached to the rear of it where he would be watch keeping. On the handover/takeover ceremony an officer handed Ritchie an aerosol horn and told him, "If any messages come over the network warning of an attack of any kind, then sound the alarm with this horn, if it is a chemical attack then sound the horn for one second on and one second off. Good luck Sergeant." And with that he was gone and he left Ritchie with a whole host of radio equipment that was squelching away and a clerk who carried the rank of Private and a look of total disdain on his face.

Poor old Ritchie knew nothing about radios or the correct voice procedure to use when using one, or as he describes voice procedure, "That funny speakey thing they do in the Royal Signals...you know, when they say hello one this another one." He looked round at the equipment that he was in charge of and didn't have a clue what he was meant to do next, so he sat in the army folding canvas chair in the corner of the tent and twiddled his thumbs all night. There were a lot of messages coming in over the radios but Ritchie didn't know if they were for him or General de la Billiere so he ignored them. He was like a fish out of water, he felt inadequate, vulnerable and useless, Ritchie says, "If Saddam

Hussein himself had walked round the corner I wouldn't even know who to go and wake up." All that money spent to train him as a soldier and it had achieved absolutely nothing.

Corporal Mick Killeen RAMC

During the reshuffle of personnel from 5 GS Regiment to 1 CS Regiment, Mick met Frank who was also a TA soldier and an ambulance crewmember. He was a 50ish rather portly bloke who was totally unsuited to the physical demands of working on a military ambulance. Mick remembers, "He used to get out of breath opening his fag packet, but he was good at other things and put this to good effect for the unit."

In civilian life Frank was a Transport Co-Coordinator for Securicor somewhere in the South of England. Frank didn't want to work on the ambulances any more so he applied to work in the unit Headquarters at Basra Palace. He was better suited to an administrative role anyway and volunteered to co-ordinate all the ambulances within 1 CS Regiment; he just applied the techniques of his civilian job to his new task. With newfound gusto, Frank set about taping Ordnance Survey maps together and placed them on a board so he could see the units' complete area of operations at a glance. All 1 CS Regiment ambulances were marked on the board by large different coloured drawing pins with their Call Signs written on the top. Each pin radiated out from the Basra Headquarters location with a matching coloured string and as the Ops Room was manned 24 hours a day, the map was constantly updated as crews radioed in their new locations. Every crewmember could instantly be located with just a quick glance at Franks' new system.

Captain Sharon Anthony QARANC

Sharon went to see the 'Friendly Fire' casualtys' Platoon Sergeant and had the following conversation,

Sharon: "Where is the soldier that shot the casualty?"

Sergeant: "You don't need to see him Ma'am, he's been dealt with."

Sharon: "I do need to see him! He is as much a casualty as the lad who was shot. Now where is he?"

Sergeant: "He's in the back of that armoured vehicle over there."

Sharon found the young lad sitting in the back of the vehicle that had been pointed out to her, the 18-year-old soldier was sobbing his heart out and had a bloody nose, no one had told him whether the soldier he had shot was dead or alive. "Did you bang your nose when you fell over?" asked Sharon. He replied, "No Ma'am, I didn't hurt myself when I fell over." He had obviously been snotted by someone within his platoon. Sharon was livid but realised this is how things are done within the infantry fraternity. He kept repeating, "I'm sorry...I am so sorry!" Sharon gave him a hug and told him not to worry because his friend was going to be all right. After spending 15 minutes reassuring the teenager he told her he was really scared because he still had to face the Regimental Sergeant Major. This fearsome man is every soldier's worst nightmare. The RSM approached the vehicle as Sharon was leaving and she told him the lad was very upset but from a medical point of view he was fit and well, the RSM gave her the impression that he wouldn't be too hard on the unfortunate soldier. The young lad was evacuated a few days later whilst Sharon reflected on the bigger impact he had on her than the soldier with the GSW (Gun Shot Wound).

Lance Corporal Matt Fairclough RAMC

Headquarters 5 GS Medical Regiment tasked 'Murph', 'Paddy', and Matt to temporarily leave 3 Para and be attached to the RAP (Regimental Aid Post) at 2 RIR (Royal Irish Regiment). They drove to the compound where 2 RIR and a prisoner of war holding camp were based. They were stopped by the guard at the compound entrance and were told to wait outside the camp gate until the CSM (Company Sergeant Major) arrived to brief them. The CSM said, "You're not one of our ambulances so you're not coming in." 'Murph' explained, "Yes we understand we're not one of your ambulances sir, but we are to be attached to your RAP and provide the necessary extra medical cover your unit has requested." The CSM was an officious type of twat and barked, "Yes, I understand what your saying Private, but I haven't received orders to that effect so you can wait here until I get word of what we are going to use you for, wait here!" Matt 'Murph' and 'Paddy' stripped off their uniforms from the waist upwards and started sunning themselves on the bonnet of their ambulance whilst they waited for the CSM to receive his orders about the mysterious medics. Ten minutes later a Chinook heavy lift helicopter carrying an army of media reporters flew into the camp to report on the Irish Regiment, the CSM came running up to the camp entrance and shouted at the guard, "The press has arrived, for fucks sake get those chavvy bastards inside the camp and hide them!" Matt heard 'Murph' grumble, "I wish you lot would make your mind up, one minute you don't want us in the camp and the next minute you do."

111

After driving into the camp and parking up behind one of the sheds; the three medics were given a ration pack to cover their feeding requirements for the next 24 hours. Twenty meters from their ambulance 300 to 400 Iraqi Prisoners of War were securely penned into a holding area by three strips of white mining tape, just the other side of the white mining tape prison was a stack of weapons ranging from pistols to 20mm cannons. A squad of Iraqi Prisoners of War were banging AK 47 magazines, full of 7.62mm ammunition, against some rocks to empty them. A single Royal Irish Regiment soldier, armed with an SA 80, was the only guard on duty watching them and the other 300 to 400 prisoners.

Sergeant Ritchie John RADC

After sitting in the CP all night doing nothing except listen to the static noises and voices on the radios, Ritchie felt very tired, but he had to wait until the CP staff arrived before he could make good his escape from this, his worst ever living nightmare. The first to arrive was a Warrant Officer from the REME (Royal Electrical and Mechanical Engineers) who strutted around the tent with an ex ranker Captain. They both annoyed Ritchie because in their arrogance they pretended he didn't exist and totally ignored him as he sat in the corner. But when a Major from the Scots Guards came in they jumped up and said, "Oh good morning sir, how are you today sir, can we get you a cup of coffee sir, could you just pull your arse cheeks a bit wider sir so I can get my tongue right up your bum." It sickened Ritchie to watch them fawn over him, and he was only a fucking Major, he also thought, 'Am I fucking invisible, I've been here all night whilst they've been tossing it off in their sleeping bags and no-one has offered to make me a cup of coffee'. That night in the CP will stay lodged in Ritchie's mind until the

112

day he dies; and it was at this point in the war that Ritchie had an epiphany.

He had learned a valuable lesson, "I probably deserved to be treated as if I was invisible, I was a nobody who knew nothing, and I needed to do something about that if I wanted to turn my life around. If you are going to take responsibility for something then you must know your gravy, you can't get through life just smiling and having a good time, you have to get things right. No one has all the right answers but in future, if I didn't have an answer to something, then I would damn well know where to get that information." It was too late for Ritchie to start learning how to be an efficient soldier, but when he did leave the army he didn't want to be that low in the food chain ever again, he wanted to be in the same position as that Major when he walked into a room. But in the future if some one did say to him, "Good morning sir, can I get you a cup of coffee," he would look in the corner of the room first, and say, "Yes please, but get your own men one first."

Corporal Mick Killeen in the back of his ambulance – note how every inch of space is used

1 CS Medical Regiment RAMC ambulances at El Almarah

Corporal Mick Killeen with Jamie Flatt's Fan – the face says it all

Mick's, Bluey's and Pally's accommodation located next to the dressing station morgue. Iraqi forces used this building during the Iran / Iraq war to torture people. Mick was never comfortable sleeping here. Bluey is the soldier standing in the doorway

Corporal Mick Killeen still carrying the fan that he was determined to insert into an orifice of Private Jamie Flatt when he got back to Wenlock Barracks

116

Captain Natalie Mehan (nee Baker) and Captain Sharon Anthony

Captain Natalie Mehan (nee Baker) and Captain Sharon Anthony

Captain Sharon Anthony

1 CS Medical Regiment RAMC location at the airfield

Parked up on the road to Basra, and waiting for orders to move forward. Just before the incident Capt Sharon Anthony witnessed with the Iraqis and their scooter

Lance Corporal Matt Fairclough in his ambulance. Note the girly picture above the stretcher

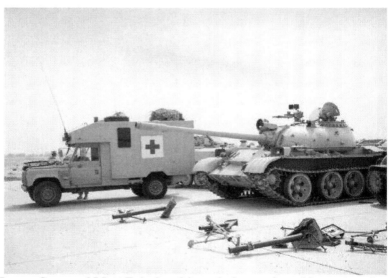

Lance Corporal Matt Fairclough's ambulance alongside captured Iraqi weaponry

Respirator checks, Lance Corporal Matt Fairclough on the right

Juliet Troop 5 GS Medical Regiment RAMC. Lance Corporal Matt Fairclough is in the middle with bush hat, Murph is wearing the shades and Paddy is standing on the far left wearing glasses

Lance Corporal Matt Fairclough and Murph digging a shell scrape

Captain Natalie Mehan (nee Baker), Captain John Batcock and Captain Sharon Anthony

Sergeant Ritchie John off to yet another O Group

Staff Sergeant Mick Germaine SQMS

Corporal Mick Killeen RAMC

It was one of those things that no one can remember how they learned about it, how do you get a cold drink whilst living in the middle of a very hot desert? British soldiers are adept at improvising and adapting to harsh conditions; US Troops would obviously put in a requisition for a refrigerator and compressor to solve the problem. The British Government is not as generous as its cousins in Washington and relies on its soldiers using their initiative. They provided plenty of plastic bottled water to all units; in fact, you couldn't swing a dead cat by its tail without hitting yet another pallet load of the stuff dumped in the barren wilderness. Mick was aware of the dangers of dehydration and kept topping his body up, but he was gagging for a really cool drink. The problem was, all the bottled water bordered on warm or hot, and drinking a lot of hot water has a laxative effect on the human body. Mick started using a very effective procedure for cooling down the bottled water, he put a bottle of water in an army sock and wet the sock with water from another bottle and then placed it in the shade but in the prevailing wind. As the wind dries out the sock it takes the heat out of the bottle and cools the water inside, after fifteen minutes you have a nice cool drink. Having to exist in the desert, Mick was learning to live with the elements and not fight or bow to them.

Captain Sharon Anthony QARANC

1 CS spent about a week at the airfield before they were given two to three hours notice to move forward, they were moving into a bombed out factory complex on the outskirts of Basra. These notices to move were given several times a day but usually ended up being cancelled; it obviously had

something to do with the constant artillery fire that was flying in and out of Basra and the Armed Sections probing up the line towards the enemy. On the day they actually moved, Sharon and her Section took down the tentage and packed all their equipment away in the vehicles, it was at this point Sharon heard a wailing sound similar to a cat being strangled.

Sharon thought the playing of military music by Regimental Bands in a war zone was one of the myths about the British Army or just a thing of the past. It was getting towards dusk and the hair on the back of Sharon's head pricked up as she looked up at the roof of one of the airfield hangars; she saw a lone bagpiper playing a lament as the sun set in the background. It was an eerie moment as the haunting music echoed around the location they were leaving; everyone stopped what they were doing and watched this young lone Scottish Piper playing his bagpipes.

The voice screaming in Sharon's head was the mother within her, her alter ego was shouting, "For Gods' sake get down from there or you will fall off and hurt yourself!"

Lance Corporal Matt Fairclough RAMC

After their stint with 2 RIR Matt and his crew returned to their previous duties of being attached to the RAP at 3 Para, the medics in the RAP were dealing with a wounded Iraqi soldier who had two gunshot wounds in his chest. The unconscious Iraqi had a chest drain inserted on the right side of his lower chest and an Intravenous Infusion in his right arm. As a couple of the 3 Para medics gave a hand to load the casualty in the back of Matt's ambulance; the patients' left arm fell off the stretcher. After placing the head end of the stretcher in the grooves that allowed it to slide into the vehicle, the Para's rammed the stretcher into the vehicle but were halted when the Iraqis' arm got caught between the ambulance and the stretcher. They pulled him back out; threw his arm on the stretcher and then pushed him all the way into the vehicle. The RMO (Regimental Medical Officer) who was supervising said, "Don't worry, he's doped up to the eyeballs and won't feel a thing, give me his treatment chart." He then wrote down and added to his previous notes; 'Possible dislocated left shoulder'.

Sergeant Ritchie John RADC

At times Ritchie was bored out of his tiny mind even during the war phase; he started working in 3 AFA's Reception and Evacuation departments just for something to do. The CDC, although still set up, seemed defunct as the Iraqis were not using chemical weapons against the coalition forces. It is a commonly known fact that the time spent on being a soldier is about 1% action and 99% boredom, Ritchie spent any time he could doing strenuous physical exercise with four other fitness fanatics within the unit. They set up a circuit training area on the edge of the location where they did sit ups, crunches, sprints, and push-ups. Ritchie really enjoyed the physical exercise as he pushed his body even harder than he did when training back in Germany. He was probably trying to make up for the boring day-to-day routine of living in the desert and not having any sex. He hated it when the unit moved location and his 'Gob Doctors' had to collapse the tents and pack away all the kit only to have to set it all up again in another God forsaken part of the desert, but at least when the unit moved they were doing something.

Staff Sergeant Bob Darkin arranged for an inter-departmental sandcastle building competition that everyone threw themselves into with great gusto; but the OC (Officer

127

Commanding) of the unit came along and told them to cease it immediately. He also decreed that there was to be no further PT sessions and the men should concentrate on the work in their individual departments; Ritchie thought the OC was worried that there might be an outbreak of morale.

Corporal Mick Killeen RAMC

The British Army had adopted the US army style cot for its soldiers to sleep on, the old fashioned British one was very close to the ground and if you leaned over to one side whilst lying on it, it catapulted you to the other side of the tent. The new style cots stood about two feet off the ground and unfolded with the legs and the thin nylon mattress incorporated into the whole contraption, it could be a pain in the arse putting it together as the material part of the cot had to be pulled taut by two bars, each at the foot and head ends. Mick had to lie down along side the nearly assembled cot, holding the middle leg and supporting the side of the cot with his neck he used his left leg to stretch the material and try to locate the small plastic lug on the end of the supporting side. Sounds simple enough, but to locate that last plastic lug when you are tired and working in temperatures over 100 degrees centigrade, it is a monumental pain in the arse. Mick had a solution.

As there was an abundance of bottled water available Mick used it to soak the nylon mattress part of his cot so it expanded and the cot could be loosely and easily assembled. Mick then left the cot under the baking sun for a couple of minutes and the nylon shrunk back to its original size and it was rigid and ready for use.

Captain Sharon Anthony QARANC

Sharon and her Section followed the rest of 1 CS from the airfield to the bombed out factory complex on the edge of Basra, they were allocated the building after the fighting armoured sections had moved forward. The building had been left in a poor state by the Black Watch Regiment who had made a point of smashing all the toilets in the undamaged parts of the factory. There was human shit all over the place and the medics had to clean it up. With the usual ingenuity that most British soldiers possess, the Section found an old galvanised dustbin and they cut out the bottom of it, placed a toilet seat on the top, and situated the whole contraption over a hole in the ground that could be filled in later. It provided a comfortable, and considering the circumstances, luxurious lavatory. Every time they moved location the galvanised toilet went with them, even if it meant strapping it onto the top of one of the Sections vehicles.

After they had arrived in the new location The Regimental Quartermaster of 1 CS sent up some medical stores to restock the sections deficiencies. The stores that arrived were all the bits and pieces they neither wanted nor requested. Sharon got the feeling that the rear echelons had all this stuff and just wanted to get rid of it and it was easier to give it to the Sections to carry, there seemed to be no sense of order or control on the re-supply system within 1 CS Medical Regiment. The one thing the Section didn't get and could have used more of was bottles of intravenous fluid. With the re-supply did come some fresh rations which were long over due as everyone had been eating compo rations since they had arrived in theatre, compo rations are high energy food but can leave the human body with degrees of constipation. The twenty soldiers within their location were given twelve bread cakes (bread rolls to any southerners reading this) and six yoghurts that had been left out in the sun and the foil tops were bulging and looked ready to burst. Any soldier stupid enough to eat these putrid rations would have had their constipation cleared within a couple of hours. One must assume that the RAMC expected Sharon to perform a five loaves and three fish's miracle with twelve bread cakes and six rancid yoghurts.

Lance Corporal Matt Fairclough RAMC

'Paddy' was knackered and wanted some extra shuteye, so Matt took over driving the ambulance whilst he slept on the stretcher in the back of the vehicle. 'Murph' was navigating the way to their next location when Matt suddenly noticed that both lanes on his side of the dual carriageway were packed with vehicles that had come to a standstill. The vehicles that were blocking the road consisted of a huge mile long convoy of US Army trucks, tanks, and armoured vehicles. Matt pulled up behind the last vehicle and jumped out to see what was causing the hold up. The convoy was so long that he and 'Murph' couldn't distinguish anything that far away. The troops escorting the US Army convoy suddenly started running around and getting into defensive positions, Matt had a .50 calibre machine gun pointed at him from the top of a Hummer vehicle. Indignantly he shouted at the US soldier on the trigger end of the weapon, "Oi! Point that fucking thing somewhere else will you, we're British Army Medics!" The Yank told him there was a roadblock up ahead and they would all have to wait in line to get through it. Matt turned off the ambulances' engine and he and 'Murph' put their weapons in the back of the ambulance with 'Paddy' before lighting up a couple of fags as they waited for the convoy to start moving again.

Fifteen minutes later two 5 GS Medical Regiment ambulances and an RMP (Royal Military Police) Land Rover, all with blue lights flashing and horns blaring, went screaming down the other side of the dual carriageway heading the way traffic should have been coming from. Matt asked the US soldier on the Hummer vehicle what was happening up ahead. The Yank had been told over the radio shortly after they had stopped that there had been a serious RTA (Road Traffic Accident) with numerous casualties requiring emergency treatment, 'Murph' shouted, "And you didn't think to tell them that there are two ambulances and crews here that could have helped." 'Murph' and Matt grabbed the crash bags and started walking up the road to see if they could help at the RTA, the Yank shouted after them, "Crazy assed Brits."

Sergeant Ritchie John RADC

The boredom wasn't the only thing that was frustrating Ritchie, he hadn't had sex for about two months, in fact the last time he had any sort of physical liaison with a woman was when he felt up a QARANC Dental Nurse under the table in an Osnabruck nightclub, and that was a week before he deployed out to Saudi Arabia. Personally running the unit porno magazine library from his tent wasn't helping much either, he had a stack of Mayfair, Penthouse and Razzle magazines that soldiers could come (Pardon the pun) and sign for in his army notebook. The rules were that each customer was only allowed one magazine at a time, could only keep it for twenty-four hours and it must be paid for up front, credit was never given in Ritchie's lending/loaning library. Payment was usually some goody or other that had been sent over by family and friends.

To relieve his own sexual frustration Ritchie would stroll over to a 4 tonner at the edge of the unit location on a Sunday night, (Sunday night was always wanking night because Ritchie thought it would be a nice way to round off the week) make sure no one was around; and give himself a quick tug. Ritchie explains, "They were all quick tugs really because I was such a state of desperation." He would then kick some sand over his…deposit, and then go back to his sleeping bag and get his head down.

Corporal Mick Killeen RAMC

The two ambulances that Mick, Bluey, Pally, and the other crew in their team were using had only one working air conditioning unit between them and unfortunately for Mick it was on the other ambulance. After a Chinese parliament involving both crews it was decided that the ambulance with the air conditioning would be used for the treatment and conveyance of casualties and the other (Poor old Mick's) used for carrying both of the crews personal kit. Mick describes his ambulance as "Looking like an old Pickford's removal truck."

The crews not only had to carry an abundance of medical kit, they also had to carry Bergen's, webbing equipment for their ammo and respirators, camp beds, sleeping bags, rations, water etc etc etc. When military ambulances are constructed for use in the field the design phase never takes into consideration the personal equipment that medics have to take with them or where to store it. They are designed to operate from a larger static unit where they can leave the majority of their personal equipment and just carry personal weapons and webbing.

After parking up for the night anyone who opened the back doors of the ambulance had to do so very carefully or they could get crushed and buried under a ton of equipment that was likely to fall out the back. Some equipment was found a specific storage place like the camp beds, they were bungeed on the bonnets of the ambulances and every nook and cranny on the vehicle was used to carry something or other. The driver of the ambulance had a handy little cubbyhole above his driving position that was large enough, with the help of some axle grease and a shoe horn, to stow a 150 Litre Bergen. Even though they were stuffed to the gunnels with equipment, they still found room for six white B & Q garden patio chairs they had purloined from a deserted Iraqi Naval Base. Never before has an RAMC ambulance resembled Jed Clampett's old Model T Ford from the TV series The Beverly Hillbillies, the only thing missing was old Granny Daisy sitting on the top in her rocking chair.

During their Chinese parliament all crewmembers came to the same decision. The ambulance carrying all their personal equipment would lead every mission, of the two vehicles, it would be better if the one not carrying any casualties drove over a buried explosive mine.

Captain Sharon Anthony QARANC

The majority of casualties received at the factory complex were a mixture of sunburn, reactions from mosquito bites, chest infections, diarrhoea, and vomiting and broken thumbs from the firing mechanisms on the Challenger tanks. One fatality also made an appearance.

A middle aged dead Iraqi civilian male was bought into Sharon's location and placed not far from the Section tent. Some of Sharon's medics and soldiers from other units

133

gathered round the body and stared at him whilst making macabre comments. Sharon lost her temper with them and shouted, "Get away from him! That is not on, he may be an Iraqi, but he is some-ones father, brother, or son, so for God's sake show some bloody respect. How would you feel if he was one of your relatives?" All the soldiers retreated and went back to their respective duties. A short while later the dead man's relatives turned up in a white transit van to collect him, they picked him up and threw him in the back of the vehicle and drove off with one of his legs hanging out the rear doors. One of the Section medics turned to Sharon and said, "Yeah! Respect Ma'am, we must make sure we always show respect!" Sharon muttered under her own breath "Smart arse."

Lance Corporal Matt Fairclough RAMC

Whilst located at Juliet Troop Headquarters all of the ambulance crews had to be on parade at 0600 hours every morning and they must have had a wash and shave and boots cleaned. The Troop Sergeant would also inspect their weapons, magazines, and ammunition to make sure they were properly cleaned and maintained. It was a routine that Matt and the others got used to in the desert, the majority of the time Matt didn't even notice he was cleaning his weapon; it was just a natural part of his life whilst out in Iraq. It was only after their Troop Sergeant was happy that they had done all of these daily routines that they were allowed to go to the chef's tent and get their breakfast.

Matt and the others had to go through a similar routine at night, they all had to report to the CP (Command Post) before last light and be briefed on passwords, NBC alert states, locations of Dressing Stations and Field Hospitals and any other information that might affect them whilst out on a shout. Everyone had to dig their own personal shell scrape near the ambulance, which they could dive into if they came under a bombardment. Matt placed his army cot along side his shell scrape so he could just roll off his cot and into it if necessary. The desert was littered with scorpions and camel spiders and they liked to crawl into sheltered areas like a soldier's boot or helmet if given the opportunity. If not on immediate standby Matt liked to take off his boots before getting into his sleeping bag to go to sleep. He would leave a rolled up sock in each of the upright boots and then placed his helmet over the top of them so they looked like a large camouflage patterned mushroom, this would prevent any creepy crawlies getting into his boots and giving him a nasty surprise in the morning. He also placed his body armour and respirator within arms reach and slept with his SA80 rifle safely tucked inside his sleeping bag with him, if the shit hit the fan at night he wanted to know exactly where all his kit was positioned.

<u>Sergeant Ritchie John RADC</u>

Discipline was beginning to slide with the soldiers in 3 AFA because they were bored and frustrated at having to live in the middle of nowhere in the desert, casualties were few and far between and in the main, the ones they did get were Iraqi soldiers with minor injuries. The temperature in the desert, especially at night, felt sub zero and was so cold that Ritchie slept inside his sleeping bag in his combat clothing and boots. Some personnel weren't even bothering to get out of their sleeping bags in time to go for breakfast.

Bob Darkin, as the head honcho of the Dressing Station, was going to give everyone in 3 AFA a good kick up the arse and get them all to start thinking and behaving like soldiers again. He got up early as usual, and after doing his ablutions and cleaning his weapon, he went round the accommodation tents and started kicking soldiers out of their sleeping bags. By the time he stormed into the 'Gob Doctors' tent Ritchie had just that very second got out of his pit, put on his helmet and webbing and was going to the latrines for a piss. The other RADC lads were still snoring their heads off when Bob started screaming, "What the fuck do you think this is, a fucking Boy Scout camp, get your fucking fat arses out of those fucking sleeping bags, and get your fucking lives sorted out!" Ritchie turned to Bob and said, "I'm glad you intervened then Bob, because they're a lazy bunch of fuckers, I've been trying to get them out of their pits for the last half an hour."

Corporal Mick Killeen RAMC

The fog of war affects everyone from the rank of Major downwards, those above that rank usually work in or occasionally attended at Divisional or Brigade Headquarters and picked up information on how the war was progressing. The majority of soldiers only knew what was happening with their own unit in a particular area of operations. Mick explains that "I had no idea where the FEBA (Forward Edge of the Battle Area) was, my geographical position meant nothing to me, I just moved from A to B and then maybe on to C in my little part of the world picking up and dropping off casualties."

The RAMC has always taught its Medics that all ambulances move forwards, a Field Hospital must collect casualties from a Field Ambulance and a Field Ambulance must do the same to collect its casualties from a units RAP (Regimental Aid Post). The old saying used to be, 'If you send an ambulance to the rear, you are losing an ambulance'. The thinking had changed and the system seemed to be a lot

136

more fluid, medics and ambulances were dispatched to where they were needed and this sometimes involved a six-hour return journey from a Field Ambulance to a Field Hospital in the rear of the battle area. Mick's Crew spent a lot of time transferring treated and stabilised casualties from his own Dressing Station to the Field Hospitals at the rear.

On one of the MSR's (Main Supply Routes) Mick and his crew came across two hard top British Army Land Rovers that were parked at the side of the road, the soldiers from the two vehicles were standing around and flapping over a casualty. The casualty was a soldier from one of the parked Rovers; he was hanging out the back of it when he lost his grip after the vehicle went over a bump in the road. He was semi-conscious and had spinal injuries.

After pulling up near the injured soldier Mick and Pally got out of their ambulance to see if they could offer any assistance. The NCO in charge came towards them and said "Fucking brilliant, how the fuck did you get here so quickly, I only sent the message on the radio a couple of minutes ago, you guys are really on the ball!" Mick Pallister took charge of the situation and the casualty was scooped up onto a spinal board and loaded into the back of the rear ambulance. The two ambulances then turned around and headed off towards the nearest Field Hospital where he was taken straight into the Operating Theatre. On their way to the Field Hospital they passed two ambulances dashing in the opposite direction with their blue lights flashing. They were too late; Mick and his crew had nicked their casualty.

Captain Sharon Anthony QARANC

Craig, the RAMC doctor who was attached to the SDG, had ordered a fridge for Sharon's Section so they could keep vaccines like anthrax and plague etc within it, electrical power for the fridge would be provided by the Sections diesel generator. The idea was to continue the vaccination programme for all British soldiers that had been initiated in BAOR (British Army Of the Rhine) and the UK prior to deploying out to the Middle East. The required fridge would need to have an accurate temperature control because being stored at an incorrect temperature could kill the vaccines; the fridge that arrived was a huge domestic type with a very flawed temperature control. Vaccines couldn't be safely stored in this particular refrigerator and so continuation of the vaccination programme was abandoned. The fridge didn't go to waste though as the Section put it on the Coldest setting and filled it with Cold drinks, and they wouldn't be parted with it for love or money.

Lance Corporal Matt Fairclough RAMC

Most Soldiers' of the British Army are a gregarious and showy lot, given half a chance they will flash their arses and genitalia to anyone who is likely to laugh or encourage them to act like an imbecile. They also have a penchant for lavatorial humour; probably from having to use communal thunderbox latrines whilst out in the field. A thunderbox is a wooden style bench with three or four holes cut into it and placed over a DLT (Deep Latrine Trench). A tent is usually put over the whole contraption to give some privacy, but you still have to drop your combat trousers and crap with two or three other soldiers sitting right next to you. It is something you get used to in the army but most soldiers would rather use the cat method of going for a shit, this involves walking a reasonable distance away from their location, at night, with a spade and a roll of toilet paper to do their business without anyone watching. Once out of sight and earshot of your comrades a small hole is dug, defecated into, and then filled in, hence calling it the cat method.

One night as Matt and 'Murph' were digging their shell scrapes 'Paddy' went of into the darkness with his shovel and roll of toilet paper, he came back fifteen minutes later and continued digging his own shelter. 'Murph' then followed suit and disappeared into the night in the same direction 'Paddy' had gone before returning to the ambulance a short while later. Matt said out loud, "Bloody hell! I've got to go now" and he then went off, their synchronised bowl movements may have something to do with eating the same compo rations at the same times. When operating as an ambulance crew you usually eat together when time is available. In the morning 'Murph' was taking in the desert view whilst cleaning his teeth and he suddenly burst into laughter and shouted, "Hey Matt! Come and have a look at this." Twenty meters from their ambulance were three piles of sand that the Coldstream Guards couldn't have lined up more perfectly.

Sergeant Ritchie John RADC

Ritchie was chatting with Lance Corporal Steve Mercer RADC in the 'Gob Doctors' accommodation tent when Bob Darkin came in with the mail, after dishing out the gratefully received envelopes and packages he looked down and saw Steve's 'farm'. "What the fuck is that?" enquired Bob. Steve was always eager to talk to anyone who had an interest in his menagerie and cheerfully told Bob, "That's my farm Staff; they are all the animals that I've managed to capture from out in the desert, they look great don't they?" Bob wasn't impressed and told Steve so, "That one is fucking dangerous you dickhead, you've got your-self a fucking Pit Viper there old son and it's poisonous, do everyone a favour and get rid of it before some one gets bitten and dies."

Corporal Mick Killeen RAMC

Mick and his crew were resting in the shade outside their cowshed style accommodation when they noticed an ambulance parking up next to their own. Driving the vehicle was a big, good-looking, black soldier called TJ, he was a Londoner, and the Crew Commander sat next to him was a 5 foot 2 inch Scottish soldier called Bobby who came from Dundee. Sitting in the front of the ambulance between these two TA soldiers was a dark-skinned woman, and she was definitely having a bad hair day. The woman was also naked and her head seemed to nod as the ambulance moved over the rough ground, she also had a large gaping mouth that seemed to be stuck in the open position.

Her latex skin was inflated to about 10 PSI and she went by the name of 'Randy Raquel', she'd been sent out to Bobby by a broadminded relative who must have purchased her from a local sex shop in Scotland. If this trio bemused the Danish troops who were guarding the compound, God only knows what the Iraqis thought of them.

Captain Sharon Anthony QARANC

The first lot of mail to be delivered to Sharon's Section arrived while they were in location at the bombed out factory and there was a great big pile of it for her personally. One of the packages was from a TA officer at 250 Field Ambulance who hadn't deployed out to Iraq, included in the parcel were some packets of crisps. Sharon kept the Walkers Chilli flavoured ones for herself because they were

140

her favourite, but she swapped some of the others with a medic in her Section who was "Gagging for a packet of crisps", in return the medic gave her a packet of biscuits she had received in the post from home.

Sharon had asked Mick to send her some packs of knickers because washing clothes whilst operating in the desert was nigh on impossible. The reason for this was because of the water discipline most soldiers have to be conscious of whilst living in the desert, it was more important for soldiers to keep their body fluids up than to keep their clothing spotlessly clean. Sharon explains, "The spare knickers were handy so that I could have a strip wash, put on clean underwear and burn the old ones with the rest of the unit waste. Mick sent clean knickers every time he put something in the post to Sharon; he sent so many of the bloody things she describes herself as "Having more knickers than dates."

Lance Corporal Matt Fairclough RAMC

'Murph' had received orders to leave their detachment at El Almarah and report back to HQ 5 GS Medical Regiment with Matt, 'Paddy' and their ambulance. The war was over and the medics from 5 GS were going to be briefed on what the plan was for their immediate future, the three of them reported to their Troop Sergeant on arrival at about 1230 hours. The Sergeant told Matt to report to the Quartermaster tent to collect his Dezzies (Desert Patterned Combat Clothing), Matt sarcastically comments, "Now the war was over it was important to get our troops in the right sort of kit for the unit photographs." The Lance Corporal Storeman in the QM's tent was obviously a very frustrated soldier because as Matt entered his domain he shouted, "And you

141

can fuck off too, you're not getting any kit because you should have been here at 1100 hours." After telling the storeman where he could shove his spare Dezzies, Matt left the tent and reported back to his Troop Sergeant and joined the others for the briefing. 5 GS Medical Regiment RAMC had orders posting them back to their barracks in Preston to train for a possible deployment out to Bosnia. That meant 'Murph' would be leaving their crew and as it turned out 'Paddy' would also be leaving, he was being discharged from his attachment to the Regular British Army and so he was now going to face the very real danger of his very angry wife. Matt was on a different list to them, he was being transferred to 1 CS Medical Regiment RAMC and would be staying out in Iraq until further notice.

'Murph' had to sign the ambulance back over to 5 GS Medical Regiment who then signed the vehicle over to Matt so that he could then drive it over to 1 CS Medical Regiment and sign it over to their unit. When 1 CS allocated Matt to a new Crew as an ambulance driver; they made him sign for one of their ambulances, it was the same one he had signed for and bought over from 5 GS Medical Regiment. God bless the British Army, in God they trust but all others must sign a fucking chit.

Sergeant Ritchie John RADC

28 Ghurkha Transport Regiment had been assigned to drive all the wheeled ambulances for 3 AFA, Ritchie, and Bob Darkin both describe them as 'Top Boys'. As 3 AFA was moving in convoy to yet another desolate part of the wilderness that is Iraq; it was noticed that one of the units' fifteen ambulances had veered off route and was heading in a 90-degree direction to the way the rest of the convoy was heading. No one could understand why the two Ghurkha

142

Drivers had broken the convoy discipline and rather dangerously headed off into the desert on their own, it must have been important but the convoy couldn't stop and wait for them.

When 3 AFA arrived at the new unit location all departments got to work setting up the departments of the Field Ambulance, this, annoyingly for Ritchie, included his damned CDC that hadn't been used for anything definitive since the pre-war Exercises.

The Land Rover ambulance and two Ghurkha Drivers that had gone astray during the unit move suddenly came into the laager area; both Drivers had big cheesy grins on their faces. After parking up they went round the back of the ambulance and took four kidnapped goats out of the stretcher carrying area, Ghurkha's are notorious for the curries they cook and curried goat is one of their specialities. The four excellent specimens they had liberated from some poor Iraqis' herd were going to give the unit a couple of fantastic fresh rations meals. Once the animals had been killed the Ghurkha's expertly butchered the carcasses ready for cooking, it was at the butchering stage that Bob Darkin pointed at the goats testicles and asked, "What are you going to do with the bollocks?" The Ghurkha Sergeant Chef replied, "We throw them away of course, they are not the best part of the animal so we don't use them." Bob asked, "Right, but they can be curried though?" The Ghurkha Sergeant confirmed that you can curry anything but they probably wouldn't taste that great. Bob instructed the Ghurkha Sergeant, "You just curry up them bad boys for me for tonight's evening meal and present them on a bed of rice."

In the cookhouse tent that night Staff Sergeant Bob Darkin placed the meal of curried goat's testicles in front of the OC of the unit saying, "Here you are sir, you've got to eat these goats bollocks." When the OC asked why he had to eat this grotesque meal, Bob told him, "The Ghurkha's see you as the Sahib, it is a great honour that they have bestowed on you, and they will deem it a personal insult to their honour if you don't eat the whole meal. In their eyes you are a great warrior and they will follow you into battle." The emotional pressure on the inexperienced RADC officer was unbearable; but because of the long tradition of Ghurkha's serving in the British Army under the command of British Officers, he felt he had no choice but to eat the goat's gonads.

It was after making the OC eat curried goat's knackers for four days on the trot that the Ghurkha Sergeant's conscience got the better of him and he told the OC, "Sahib, you don't have to eat any more." If Ritchie and Bob had had their way, the OC would have been eating them for breakfast.

Corporal Mick Killeen RAMC

During the journey to deliver a casualty to a Field Hospital the medic in the rear of the ambulance had to assess and treat all injuries, and any treatment, drugs or IV fluids given to the casualty had to be noted on his treatment card. The medic also had to label the casualty's personal equipment with the correct name, rank, number and unit, the casualty's kit is then held by the QM Department at the hospital ready for collection when either returning to his unit or evacuated back to the UK. All casualties are assessed as either Priority 1, 2 or 3 so they can be treated in order of urgency when admitted to the hospital. A Priority 1 obviously takes precedence over any of the Priority 2's and 3's.

144

On approaching the Field Hospital all ambulances would be stopped by the hospitals' Infantry Security Company, they would identify both ambulances as friendly forces. Mick would shout to the guard in the Sanger, "We've got one Priority 1 stretcher case and two walking Priority 2 cases!" The guard in the Sanger would then telephone Reception and tell them what category of casualties were on their way, the Reception Staff would then be outside waiting for the ambulance to drive the 500 meters up to the hospital. Mick reflects, "34 Field Hospital RAMC were really on the ball every time we tipped up at their Reception."

As the casualty was dropped off at Reception the medic briefed the Field Hospital staff on all the details pertaining to the casualty and his injuries, then the casualty's kit was dropped off at the QM's. Lastly the ambulance crew had to call at the hospital armoury that was housed in a large metal shipping container; the Hospital Infantry Security Company also administered this. They handed in any weapons, ammunition, grenades and bayonet that the casualty was carrying. The weapons Butt and Serial Numbers were logged in a register, along with the Number Rank and Name of the soldier it was assigned to, before being placed onto a rifle rack. All rounds were taken out of their magazines and put in an empty Hessian sandbag before being handed over, as there were thousands of rounds of ammunition handed in every day they were logged in under the amount 'various'. Mick lost count of the thousands and thousands of rounds he had handed in every time they dropped off a casualty, something he would remember when he came to hand in his own ammo at the end of the tour. If the soldier returned to his unit after treatment, he would collect his personal weapon from the armoury, if evacuated back to the UK; the weapon would remain in the armoury.

Captain Sharon Anthony QARANC

The Collecting Sections moved forward again as the Iraqi forces retreated further into the city of Basra, this time Sharon's location was in a college on the outskirts of the city. It was a new building that had suffered some bomb damage and resulted in most of the windows being blown out, remarkably the large sliding reception doors were intact but not working. The reception area was large enough to be used by the Section as a triage centre, this would be where all the casualties received into the unit could be checked over and prioritised before treatment began. On receiving the following casualties they would have to assess which one would be treated first, second and third:

1. A British soldier with trauma to both lower legs.
2. An Iraqi enemy soldier with severe burns to both hands.
3. An unconscious child.

Medics have to rise above the instinct to 'treat our own first' and should deal with the casualty that is in the most critical condition. If the child is not breathing and the British soldier's bleeding has been stemmed then an attempt to resuscitate the child must take priority, however, if the child is breathing and the soldier had an arterial bleed then setting up an Intravenous Infusion on the British soldier must take priority after arresting his bleeding. Now, throw into this conundrum the Iraqi enemy soldier with the severe burns to his hands, lets say he has also suffered inhalation burns to his larynx and needs a plastic airway inserted. He is the enemy and may have caused the injuries sustained by the British soldier in the next treatment bay, how are you going to feel about having to treat him first? The medics have to decide which casualty to treat first regardless of age, sex, colour, creed or popularity, all the casualties need help and amid the hysteria and screams medical personnel have to set their own emotions aside, and when the Dressing Stations are overloaded to bursting point, the medics alone must decide who lives and who dies.

In one of the admin offices at the side of the reception area Sharon and her team found undisturbed desks, chairs and paperwork, it was like the Marie Celeste, the occupants of the building seemed to have just got up from their desks and walked out of the building. As they cleared the undamaged furniture away to make room for the treatment bays for incoming casualties, Sharon found some student ID cards, certificates and course work that was awaiting marking. Looking at the photos of the students on the ID cards really personalised the war for Sharon, some of them were about the same age as her own children and she wondered where they were at that particular moment in time. Things seemed to be very quiet since Sharon and her Section had moved into the college, they had received some casualties but the fighting had died down a bit, it seemed the Iraqis had lost the will to fight. The medics were about to get a wake up call.

Lance Corporal Matt Fairclough RAMC

A TA Sergeant called Carol was to be Matt's new Crew Commander whilst he was attached to 1 CS Medical Regiment, her fiancé Pete, a TA Corporal, was appointed as the Medic of their crew whilst Matt would be the driver. Before they left Headquarters 1 CS Medical Regiment and headed back up to El Almarah, Corporal Mick Killen told Matt some information about Carol that he thought he should know. "She is a fucking pain in the arse to work with mate, she has bitched non stop about the last three drivers on

147

her crew, so much so, that they keep replacing them just to shut her up. You will get the DCM for this mate, I don't mean the Distinguished Conduct Medal, I mean the Driving Carol Medal, good luck." Matt wasn't surprised to learn that back in her civilian life Carol was an Advanced Driving Instructor.

As Matt started to drive away from their new units' Headquarters, Matt pulled out a Benson and Hedges cigarette from the top pocket of his combat jacket and picked up his lighter from the dashboard, Carol sneered, "You don't think I'm going to allow you to smoke in this ambulance do you?" A line had just been drawn in the sand and Matt just had to cross it. He told her, "Listen Carol, the front of this vehicle is my home from home, you're in charge of the back of this vehicle and I definitely won't smoke in there if you so wish, but I am going to smoke in my own front room." Matt then lit up and smoked the first of many cigarettes driving his ambulance whilst earning his DCM.

Sergeant Ritchie John RADC

The war had started about twenty-four hours earlier and up to this point 3 AFA hadn't received any casualties, if there were any casualties up at the FEBA then they must have been tended by one of the other Field Ambulances. In the early hours of the morning a duty Sergeant at 3 AFA's Reception was studiously reading his CTR's (Casualty Treatment Regimes – an aide memoir for RAMC personnel), he was doing some last minute cramming in case some casualties did start coming into the unit. Just then an SAS soldier came bursting into the reception area holding a terrified and scrawny Iraqi Prisoner Of War by the scruff of the neck; the Iraqi soldier was covered in cuts and bruises

148

and had obviously been treated quite firmly by the British Army's finest. The tough looking SAS soldier's face was covered in green and black cam cream and he was carrying an M16 assault Rifle, on his specialist webbing he carried a 9mm pistol, fighting knife, and an assortment of equipment. Still holding his poor wretch of a prisoner by the scruff of the neck, the Special Forces hero lifted the Iraqi's head up and presented it to his audience like a puppet at a Punch and Judy show, "Where do you want this one Jon?" growled the hero. The Duty Medic Sergeant was a bit taken aback by the dramatic entrance of this dynamic one and a half, so he instructed that the prisoner be placed in one of the Receptions' canvas chairs. The Reception team went to work processing the enemy soldier by checking his medical status and vital signs, the Reception Sergeant turned to question the mysterious British Special Forces Warrior to find out why he had bought him into 3 AFA. But like the Red Shadow in the 1920's black and white film; the hero had suddenly and silently vanished back into the wilderness of the desert.

Corporal Mick Killeen RAMC

It was not unusual for the ambulance crews to be surrounded by local inhabitants when they were picking up or dropping off casualties. The children in particular seemed to be fascinated by anything 'Military'. Since time began, young boys of all nations around the world have always been attracted to army vehicles and soldiers carrying weapons.

A coincidence of being swamped by these indigenous people was the fact that they would try to steal anything that wasn't bolted down. It didn't matter whether it was of any use to them or not, the fact that it was there was a good enough reason to pilfer it. Mick grabbed a young lad, who was

149

trying to make a get away with a tube of KY Jelly; maybe the mischievous scamp was considering setting up his own gynaecological clinic.

The child's father was also there and apologised profusely for his sons transgression, he was obviously embarrassed by the fact that his son had stolen from the very people who were there purely and simply to help his country. The Iraqi father said to Mick, "I am so sorry for what my son has done to you, he has offended you greatly, and the imbalance must be corrected. I will take him home immediately and beat his mother!" The Iraqi philosophy of life is that if a son does something wrong, it is his mothers fault. Mick had a mental image of the poor Iraqi mother receiving another thrashing and thinking, 'Oh no, what has the little sod done now for me to deserve this'.

Captain Sharon Anthony QARANC

An infantry Section positioned on the outskirts of Basra was going to have a brew at 0100 hours; a young 18-year-old soldier was about to pour the boiling water into his comrade's mugs and finish making the tea for everyone. In the British Army the youngest soldier in a Section is always known as the 'Brew Bitch'. It was very dark and the Section was about to settle down for the night, presumably after everyone had been allocated his stag (Period of duty) on sentry through the night. Suddenly they were attacked by some Iraqi soldiers who assaulted the Section with grenades and small arms fire, in the resulting mayhem the British soldiers gathered their wounded into the Warrior AFV and battened down the hatches, they knew the location of Sharon's Collecting Section and headed straight for it.

The warrior came charging into the Collecting Sections location and dramatically halted outside the triage area at the college, responsibility for everything then immediately transferred from the infantry to the medics. There were two seriously wounded in the Section and they were assessed and taken into the treatment bays so life-saving procedures could be started, about six unwounded soldiers from the section were in a state of shock and the medics put them all together in a side room away from the screams of their two comrades in the treatment bays. The medics put blankets round the infantrymen, gave them hot sweet tea, and tried to reassure them that their friends were going to be all right. Sharon noticed that some of her own young medics looked pale and horrified by what was occurring around them and what they had to deal with.

In the treatment bays, Craig the RMO (Regimental Medical Officer), and Sharon took command of the treatment regimes of the two seriously wounded soldiers, wounds were dressed, morphine and antibiotics injected and at the same time oxygen and Intravenous fluids were set up and administered. The more experienced RAMC medics and RMA's (Regimental Medical Assistants) from the Irish Guards were involved with the treatment of the severely wounded, this involved assisting the RMO when he inserted chest drains to clear blood out of the casualties damaged lungs. Craig and Sharon supervised and advised each of the medics as they simultaneously carried out their individual tasks to try and keep these soldiers alive. The RMA's and Dave, Sharon's CMT 1 Lance Corporal, were all very good but inexperienced and naïve. They had trained on Exercise with simulated casualties but this was a whole different thing, luckily Craig and Sharon had a wealth of medical emergency experience between them, albeit in Accident and Emergency Departments in the UK. The 18-year-old lad who was making the brews when the Section was attacked was also injured, his hands were badly scalded and he had shrapnel wounds on his hands and fingers. Another group of medics from Sharon's team started treating him in the Primary Care Section, the first thing they had to do was calm him down, he kept sobbing over and over again, "I want to go home...let me go home...tell me this isn't happening!" He was in such a severe state of shock and distress that it took him 24 hours to calm down from his ordeal.

Whilst these frantic scenes were being played out the Collecting Section Sergeant, along with a Corporal and a couple of RAMC Privates, went out to the Warrior AFV to collect the bodies of two British soldiers from the infantry section who had been killed during the ambush. There were no body bags to put them into so the Sergeant improvised and used a couple of NBC (Nuclear Biological and Chemical) casualty bags. NBC casualty bags are made from an NBC proof material that a casualty can be sealed into it to protect him from any chemical vapour hazard, the manufacturers boast that a casualty can breathe safely without using his respirator once sealed in the bag. The NBC casualty bags are roughly the same size as a body bag and sufficed until some proper ones were obtained. Dog tags had to be taken off the dead and documentation and personal effects had to be removed and put into an envelope and sealed, all the casualties' personal effects, weapons and equipment were handed over to the 1 CS's Regimental Quartermasters Department. To have to go through the pockets of a dead comrade must be one of the grimmest jobs any soldier has to carry out. Sharon remembers "We were so lucky to have the Padre Captain Ian Richardson with us, not only did he do such a great job of comforting the shocked and wounded but he also helped to deal with the dead as well."

The severely injured soldiers were treated and evacuated by wheeled ambulances within 45 minutes of the Warrior AFV driving into the triage location but the two dead soldiers remained in a side room until they could be removed the following day.

All of the wounded and dead were treated with a great deal of dignity and reverence.

Lance Corporal Matt Fairclough RAMC

At an airfield a couple of miles outside Basra; Matt and his crew were temporarily working from a Medical Centre; outside the building there were four 1 CS Medical Regiment ambulances neatly parked up side by side. Whilst things were quiet the crews sunbathed in some old chairs they'd found and although they were enjoying the rest; just hanging around and doing nothing was very boring. Some US Army soldier's interrupted the medic's quiet time; one was a Master Sergeant who was some sort of medically trained bloke and the other was a young black female PFC (Private First Class- the equivalent rank in the British Army would be Lance Corporal) who was an army driver. The Master Sergeant asked, "Can we have a look round your ambulances, they look neat." Matt gave them a guided tour and the Master Sergeant was particularly interested in the medical kit in the rear of the ambulance and was impressed when shown the defibrillator and all the other gadgets. The PFC asked how the ambulance handled when driving "A stick vehicle" referring to the fact that it wasn't an automatic gearbox, which most US Army vehicles are. Matt asked her if she wanted a cabby and she jumped at the chance, he ran through the controls with her and after five minutes instruction she pulled away from the Medical Centre and revved the guts out of first gear, Matt urged her to change up

153

to second before the gearbox fell out the bottom of his vehicle. They headed down the unused runway and the excited PFC went up through the gears and took the ambulance up to its maximum speed of 70 MPH. On returning to the Medical Centre she said, "Hell that was good, our Hummers ain't that fast, they're all governed to 50 MPH."

The Yanks returned the favour and let the British medics look over their Hummer medical vehicle which was very basic; in the rear of it there was just a stainless steel scoop stretcher and a backboard. The Master Sergeant explained that their role only came into play if a US Medevac helicopter couldn't land near a casualty; they would scoop up the casualty on the stretcher and shoot out of the area and deliver him to the chopper at a safe location. The British medics were not impressed.

Sergeant Ritchie John RADC

Ritchie had done nothing constructive or useful within 3 AFA since the unit had arrived in Saudi and Iraq, even working temporarily in Reception and Evacuation had done nothing to alleviate his boredom, there was barely enough work for the guys who were supposed to be working in those departments. Apart from a couple of dispatch riders from the AAC (Army Air Corps), who had fallen off their motorbikes in the dark and fractured a couple Scapula's and a Humerus, there had been very few casualties coming through their unit. Ritchie plainly states, "The only other patients we saw was a soldier with a cough, one with a Cold and an officer with a very bad case of verruca's. We didn't even get the chance to use the mobile dental kit because we didn't receive any dental patients."

The first and only casualty they did receive with trauma injuries was brought into Reception and he caused a bit of a fuss, all the medics wanted to get involved and carry out the job they were trained to do. The casualty was a 40 year old Iraqi soldier who'd had a leg blown off and had been left unattended and alone in the desert. Remarkably he had saved his own life by managing to dress the stump of his severed limb using an empty sandbag and a roll of masking tape, a couple of British soldiers spotted him near a destroyed Iraqi APC (Armoured Personnel Carrier) and bought him into 3 AFA in their Land Rover. As the medics went to work on him with IV's, painkillers and antibiotics, a lot of the other unit members turned up with their cameras and started taking pictures of the bewildered Iraqi soldier.

Co-located with 3 AFA was 23 PFA (Parachute Field Ambulance) who had an MST (Mobile Surgical Team) attached to them and they had a twenty five-bed ward, x-ray facilities and an Operating Theatre. The Airborne medics were as bored as their counterparts in 3 AFA, but because they had more medical facilities than 3 AFA, the prized casualty had to be handed over for life saving surgery. Once the Iraqi soldier had been handed over, everyone went back to being bored.

Corporal Mick Killeen RAMC

"You could smell Basra from 10 Kms away, it smelled of bad eggs and vegetables," says Mick. His crew had set up in one of Saddam's old palaces and Mick noticed that because of the lack of fuel available to the civilian population, some of the old large vehicles used by the Iraqi's had their engines and bonnets removed and were pulled along by a couple of donkey's. Some of the car boots opened up like a motorcar from the 1920's to reveal seats that two passengers could

155

travel in on the outside of the vehicle, these were usually occupied by two women in full Muslim black headdress whilst the back and front seats of the car were crammed full of goats. The only position inside the car occupied by anyone who wasn't a domesticated mammal with horns was the driver, and he was only there to steer the vehicle.

As Mick travelled up and down the MSR's (Main supply Routes) he also noticed Iraqi women walking around with large bundles of wood on their heads or carrying large plastic containers of water. They worked very hard even during the very hottest part of the day whilst the men folk sat in the shade on their haunches, smoking, drinking and putting the world to rights with their neighbours. It also amazed Mick that the Iraqi children left their squalid mud hut type homes and traipsed off to school in immaculate uniforms, all white clothing worn by the kids looked like an advert from a Persil TV commercial.

Captain Sharon Anthony QARANC

One of the RAMC Private medics in Sharon's Section was a 20-year-old Zimbabwean girl whose brother was also serving in Iraq, but he was up in the frontline in one of the British fighting regiments. Sharon and the Padre had the onerous task of telling her that one of the soldiers killed in the warrior ambush was her brothers' best friend. Sharon can't remember the dead soldiers name but in a photograph line up of soldiers killed in Iraq, the ones the media love to display on television, she can easily pick him out. The British Army pulled her brother away from his unit and sent him to a rear area where he spent 24 hours with his sister; she was given the heavy burden of breaking the bad news to her brother.

Lance Corporal Matt Fairclough RAMC

Iraqi civilians kept turning up at 2 RTR's (Royal Tank Regiment) RAP (Regimental Aid Post) with a variety of injuries and illnesses but all of the RAMC's RMO's (Regimental Medical Officer) had been given strict instructions to turn them all away. Unfortunately the local Iraqi hospitals' didn't even have any basic medical kit to deal with at least minor injuries, and one particular RMO was finding it difficult to come to terms with obeying his military orders and going against his Hippocratic oath. These people needed help and he wasn't allowed to give it.

An Iraqi doctor approached the troubled RMO and asked if the British Army could at least help him out with some basic medical supplies for his hospital, he could then give some sort of treatment to those in need. The RMO and Matt went on a Recce in Matt's ambulance taking the Iraqi doctor with them to the local hospital; he wanted to see for himself how bad their situation was, the hospital was located in the centre of the town about five minutes drive away from his RAP. It was as bad as the Iraqi doctor had said and the RAMC RMO (who shall remain nameless) said to Matt, "Fuck it! These people need help, let's at least give them the means to help themselves." On returning to his RAP the RMO begged, stole and borrowed a mass of medical stores that he, Carol, Pete and Matt loaded into the ambulance and delivered to the local Iraqi hospital. The bulk of the stores they handed over were, IV fluids, giving sets, cannulas, bandages, dressings and micropore sticky tape. The RMO wanted to help out as much as he could but insisted that the hospital was not given any drugs or ointments.

Sergeant Ritchie John RADC

Before the war had started, a team of soldiers within 3 AFA decided to start writing a skit magazine to raise morale and somewhat relieve the boredom of the medics. The editorial team consisted of Staff Sergeant Bob Darkin, Corporal Willy Wilson RAMC, and Corporal Chris Scard RAMC; Sergeant Ritchie John RADC joined the team, as a consultant to make sure each edition wasn't too boring, he was considered, apparently, an expert on all things dull. The unit magazine was entitled B.O.N.K. which stood for; Better Off Not Knowing, and it was full of satirical news reports about the war, soldiers in 3 AFA, and some of the incidents that had occurred in recent days. Issue one was created in Saudi Arabia whilst waiting for the big push and Bob Darkin ironically points out that, "The war was so short we only managed five issues." The magazine was a smaller version of a newspaper entitled 'The Wipers Times' that was locally produced by soldiers in the Ypres Salient during the First World War, but both B.O.N.K and 'The Wipers Times' achieved their aims in raising morale, B.O.N.K. was definitely more graphic, lewd and crude though.

The Chief Clerk of 3 AFA joyfully received a copier machine and printer so he could produce Part One Orders (Typed routine orders that are displayed daily in every department informing everyone in the unit of parades and meal timings etc) for the unit, Captain MacDonald the Senior Nursing Officer got permission for the editorial team to reproduce copies of B.O.N.K. on the copier so they could be distributed in greater numbers. The first edition was produced on a computer that was linked to the copier and printer; but after just a couple of copies the machinery packed up due to sand and dust getting into the gadgets mechanism, and it never worked again. For a while the printing gizmos were left in the corner of a trailer until some one decided it was unwanted baggage and buried it in the desert along with forty unwanted and ancient Thomas Splints.

The team resorted to making up the magazine with hand written reports and some wonderful, but sometimes monstrous, drawings that were provided by Corporal Willy Wilson RAMC. The entire team worked through the night in the Minor Treatments bay to ensure the next edition was available in the morning; they had to write up the stories, and complete the drawings ready for people to read it in the morning. It was impossible to produce more than one copy though without a photocopier, so the edition they produced was left in the Reception tent and was made available for everyone to read.

Corporal Mick Killeen RAMC

Mick's crews were on the MSR heading back to their Dressing Station at El Almarah after completing another routine job; he noticed the increased oncoming traffic included a British armoured column whose commander was giving them the thumbs up sign. The ambulance crew just thought he was being friendly. Out of his passenger side window Mick could see the distant village of Majar al Kabir and his attention was drawn to a lot of helicopter activity flying above and around that area, he hadn't seen that many choppers flying since the war had ceased.

They were over taken by two large civilian pickup trucks carrying young Iraqi men wearing Shemag's that covered their faces. They all stared at Mick and Bluey with suspicion and hostility as they slowly overtook. Mick cocked his SA 80 rifle and shouted to Mick Pallister in the back of the ambulance, "Pally! You better get ready; I think something's going to kick off in a minute!" The two pickup trucks pulled away into the distance whilst the men in the back continued to stare menacingly.

A short distance later they approached the Sanger at the entrance to their camp and Mick saw what could only be described as mayhem, they pulled up outside the building that housed their Dressing Station, and heard SNCOs shouting orders and medical personnel sprinting to God knows where. Mick was oblivious to the fact that six RMP (Royal Military Police) NCOs had just been murdered at Majar al Kabir in a small isolated police station. NCOs and Officers were shouting and screaming orders to anyone standing around doing nothing. Someone shouted at Mick, "Go to the helipad! Go! Go! Go!" A Chinook heavy lift helicopter was on the helipad with its rotor blades still turning, Mick passed four soldiers heading back towards the Dressing Station carrying a casualty on a stretcher. The Chinook was empty and Mick was waved off by one of the aircrew, he doubled back to catch up with the men carrying the casualty and took over from one of them, they all seemed totally knackered. A Para Field Ambulance vehicle came screaming up to the Dressing Station with a dead soldier on board, someone was crying out "Help my mate, for Christ's sake someone help him!" The noise, confusion, and sense of urgency had made the incident traumatic and distressing but Mick never panicked, he just did as he was told even though he didn't really understand what had happened. Like the NBC drills, in an emergency situation, soldiers go into an automotive style of action.

When everything had quietened down Mick helped carry the dead to the temporary morgue that was located next to his accommodation. He thought sleeping next door to the temporary morgue was macabre, but the Dressing Station had to put the dead soldiers from the police station somewhere. The same night the murders had taken place Captain Ruth Pollendine QARANC (a nursing officer also from 250 Hull) and three RAF Auxiliary nurses started cleaning up the bodies of the murdered RMP soldiers. The nurses' gently cleaned mud and dirt from the soldier's faces and bodies, they used clean water and cotton triangular bandages as flannels. Mick and his crew went into the morgue to give the nurses a hand but felt they were just getting in the way; they were making a difficult job even harder. An RAF nurse followed Mick outside carrying a metal bowl of bloody water and she poured it into a burning trench. The burning trench was about the size of a grave and all medical refuse from the Dressing Station was dumped in it, when the trench was full, it was soaked in diesel, then set on fire and incinerated.

As Ruth and her colleagues continued with their gruelling task an SIB (Special Investigation Branch) Officer and Staff Sergeant from the RMPs entered the morgue. When they saw what Ruth and the other nurses were doing, the SIB officer went ape shit and started shouting about the bodies being a 'Crime Scene' that should be left undisturbed. Ruth calmly replied, "I am not a police officer, I am a nursing officer and I am just doing my job! I obviously won't treat this as a 'Crime Scene' until someone tells me!" A lack of communication between separate branches of the British Army must have left both the Military Police Officers and Ruth, feeling frustrated and angry.

The following day Mick's ambulance was one of three that were detailed to carry the six RMP bodies from the Morgue to a waiting Chinook helicopter. Two bodies were put on each ambulance and they were driven slowly through the camp to the helipad, as they drove past the cookhouse every soldier stood silent and perfectly still as a mark of respect. The silence on the camp was unnerving; Mick felt like a hearse driver and could feel the hair on the back of his neck stand up.

The feeling on the camp was one of anger and hostility, Mick comments, "3 Para were all bombed up and ready to go out and seriously fuck up everyone's day." For some reason known only to the 'Top Knobs' all troops were stood down and no retribution was taken, on reflection it was probably a good idea as angry paratroopers make a hell of a mess. Mick and his crew also felt angry at the atrocity, "We were out there to help them, and they fucking murdered some of our lads."

The ambulance crews started driving aggressively, to the extent that the local Iraqi's sometimes had to leap for their lives as ¾ ton Land Rover ambulances tried to run them down. When the local civilians watched and stared as they passed by, Mick and his crew would scowl at them shouting, "What are you fucking looking at!" They started travelling around with weapons cocked and safety catches on, Mick was almost willing the locals to give him an excuse to open fire. This was not the same Mick that left Hull five months previously, he used to be the most placid, sociable, and funny man you could meet. Now he was angry, unafraid and dangerous, he and his mates even talked about how they could possibly kill some Iraqi's and get away with it.

The operational tour was taking its toll on Mick.

Captain Sharon Anthony QARANC

The day after the Warrior incident Sharon debriefed her Section on what had happened, what the medics had done, why they did it and how they could improve on the procedures they might have to go through again. Within two days the Section left the college location and moved into a University building closer to the centre of Basra. It was an old building and quite dark inside which gave the location a depressive atmosphere. A lot of units were co-located in the same area; a POW (Prisoner of War) holding Section was one of the units and as well as holding POW's it held civilians who had been caught looting homes and shops.

Inside the main doors of the building was a large hallway; at the far end was a library and doors off the corridor led to the classrooms. Sharon was allocated the English Department to work in and whilst setting up their equipment she noticed the walls were decorated with the poems of William Wordsworth and some of Shakespeare's most famous quotations. Underneath these very English words someone from the Iraqi government had printed, "These are the words of the almighty Saddam Hussein."

Lance Corporal Matt Fairclough RAMC

Matt hadn't actually seen any fighting whilst out in Iraq, the nearest he came to any danger was when a scud missile landed near his location with 3 Para. It was nightfall and the lads were sleeping in their shell scrape when the ensuing explosion and flash of light woke them all up. They masked up whilst still lying in their sleeping bags; and then went back to sleep. Forty-five minutes later a Para woke them up and told them they could unmask as there wasn't any chemical threat, they unmasked, and then went back to sleep again. In the morning Matt 'Murph' and 'Paddy' went to have a look at the massive shell hole that was about one hundred meters from the 3 Para location. Although he hadn't seen any action, Matt had seen the results of the fighting and was involved most days in moving the wounded from RAP's to Dressing Station's to Field Hospitals.

One day whilst at 5 GS Medical Regiment Headquarters which was located at one of Saddam Hussein's Palaces, Matt was standing in the massive foyer and noticed his unit had set up a large flat screen television set that was constantly showing Sky TV News programmes. The Sky News footage was of coalition aircraft taking off from aircraft carriers and airbases in Saudi Arabia, coalition bombs exploding in Baghdad, Abram tanks moving through the desert and US Marines shooting erratically at some poor bastard. Matt was mesmerised by the Television and what was happening on the screen, he said, "Bloody hell! When did all this happen?"

Sergeant Ritchie John RADC

Staff Sergeant Bob Darkin nabbed Lance Corporal Steve Mercer about the rather dangerous Pit Viper snake that was in his menagerie, "Have you got rid of that snake yet?" Steve casually told Bob that he had indeed extracted the poisonous reptile from his 'farm' and was in fact sad to see his favourite pet leave. When Bob asked what he had done with the venomous creature, Steve calmly told him he had put it in the OC's sleeping bag. When Bob pointed out that he could be convicted of murder if the OC died from his pets' snakebite, Steve just shrugged his shoulders and walked off.

Corporal Mick Killeen RAMC

The RSI (Regimental Signals Instructor) from HQ 1 CS Medical Regiment was visiting Mick and his crew's detachment in an FFR (Fitted For Radio) Land Rover, he was there to inspect an ambulance radio and deliver some spare batteries. Sergeant Paul Greensides RAMC was driving the accompanying Shotgun Land Rover because his own ambulance crewmembers were ill and his crew had been taken off the road. He was deemed a 'Spare Bod' and with nothing better to do he volunteered to 'ride shotgun' for this detail and visit his mate Mick Killeen.

They had both served in 250 Field Ambulance for over twenty years, and done countless Military Exercises and Annual Summer Camps together. Mick even knew of Paul before joining the TA because he had been in Mick's older brothers' class at school in Beverley. The RSI was busy in the location all day, so Paul spent this time drinking tea and catching up on what Mick had been doing since he had last seen him.

If you drove like a bat out of hell it was a two-hour journey back to the Regimental Headquarters in Basra and as the sun was starting to dip over the horizon, the RSI was getting fidgety about getting back. The war was over but thin-skinned vehicles were not allowed to travel unescorted after dark, it was felt there was no need to take unnecessary risks.

On his own, Paul drove the Land Rover out of the location and followed the RSI who headed south towards Basra. As they got onto the long straight road through the desert, Paul accelerated hard and followed the FFR as it overtook a Danish Medical Team travelling in convoy. The Danish convoy was carrying a full surgical team who had radio contact with a helicopter casevac (Casualty Evacuation) system. After passing the Danish convoy a front tyre blew out on Paul's Land Rover, and it crashed off the road and rolled over and over and over. Paul wasn't wearing a seat belt.

Mick was notified there had been an RTA not far from their location but they were not to respond as a Danish Medical Team was dealing with it. Mick was quite pleased as he could now head off and hit the hay. The following day Mick saw the mangled wreckage of Paul's Land Rover after it had been recovered by the REME (Royal Electrical and Mechanical Engineers) into his location. He said out loud, "Fuck me! That's one of our Rovers." It took a couple of seconds before he realised that the vehicle was the same one Paul was driving the day before. "Oh no, it's fucking Paul's! Oh God, not Paul. Not now, not after all this!" The squaddie grapevine was not helping either as tales of the drivers' fate ranged from him being crushed to death, to a total decapitation.

Frantic messages were sent to HQ 1 CS Medical Regiment to ascertain exactly what had happened to Paul. A Radio Operator from 1 CS came out and made a statement to Mick and the other ambulance crews, "This is fact, Sergeant Paul Greensides was in an RTA yesterday evening and as the Rover rolled he was thrown through the roof canopy. He was treated by a Danish Medical Team that was following him on the MSR; he has a fractured shoulder and is currently sitting up in bed in 32 Field Hospital enjoying some tea and toast." Mick's relief was overwhelming and when he went to visit him at 32 Field Hospital, Paul told him he could remember nothing of the accident. Mick believes that because the Danish Medical Team were on the spot when the accident happened, someone, somewhere was looking down and saying, "Not today Paul…not today."

Captain Sharon Anthony QARANC

The Iraqi Prisoners of War were held in a compound near Sharon's collecting Section, and even though they were well treated by the British Army, it was crowded and uncomfortable in the holding compound. Word got round the Iraqi prisoners that if they feigned an illness they would be taken to a British Army medical unit to be medically examined, and in doing this they could temporarily escape the compound and they might even get some sort of preferential treatment.

An Irish Guardsman armed with an SA 80 rifle bought the prisoners that were complaining of being unwell into the collecting Section under escort. Very few of the prisoners spoke enough English to be understood and each of them was usually wailing at the top of his voice whilst flailing his arms and legs about. When they realised Sharon, a mere woman, was going to examine them, the histrionics went into overdrive. Sharon says, "Nine times out of ten they behaved like drama queens and there was actually nothing wrong with them. The Iraqi prisoners were so frustrating to deal with that I actually threw a cup of water in one of their faces just to get him to calm down." Sharon to this day is mortified by her own behaviour, "It was unprofessional to say the least and not the standard of care you would expect from a British Nurse, if I had done that to a patient in a UK hospital I would have been sacked on the spot. It did shock the patient though and he calmed down enough for me to examine him and realise he wasn't ill, and I sent him back to the prisoner compound."

Sharon had been through a lot since deploying out to Iraq and she had taken a lot of crap, even from her own comrades, and yet she still beats herself up for throwing a cup of water at someone.

Lance Corporal Matt Fairclough RAMC

Matt and Kirsty had been divorced for six months before he had deployed out to Iraq and although he had his decree absolute; their solicitors hadn't worked out the final settlement. The matrimonial home and contents were to be given to Kirsty as Matt didn't want anything from their marriage; he agreed she could have everything. The only problem was that Matt had to sign the deeds of the house over to Kirsty before she could sell the place; and a young couple definitely wanted to buy the house in Driffield. Kirsty contacted the Chief Clerk of 250 Field Ambulance in Wenlock Barracks to ask for Matt's address out in Iraq so she could send the deeds out for him to sign. For security reasons the Chief Clerk refused to give Matt's address to her but said she would contact Matt and ask if he would consent to the unit letting his ex wife know where he was located. Matt refused and left instructions that Kirsty would have to take the deeds to his dad's house in Beverley and Harry would forward them to him out in Iraq. He also demanded that a stamped addressed return envelope should also be included with the deeds as there weren't many stationery shops or post offices out in the desert.

When the document arrived at 5 GS Medical Regiment it didn't have the stamped addressed envelope enclosed; so Matt had to fashion an envelope big enough to hold the document, and he borrowed an old second-class stamp that 'Murph' found in the crease of his wallet. By the time the

168

deeds got back to Kirsty in Driffield the sale of the house was lost, 'All for the want of a first class stamp'.

Sergeant Ritchie John RADC

The RCT (Royal Corps of Transport) drivers of 3 AFA's 4-ton wagons offered Ritchie the chance of having a cabby in an MK 4 tonner. Ritchie has always been bored shitless about anything to do with weapons and military vehicles, but he was so mind numbingly bored with his life out in the desert, he jumped at the chance. He was given a couple of minute's instruction on the controls before the RCT driver, who was sitting in the passenger seat, allowed him to speed off into the desert and drive the military vehicle for a while. Unfortunately Ritchie has a very low attention span and he soon became bored with the experience even though the RCT soldier was quite impressed with his desert driving skills. Ritchie must have picked up the aptitude from his dad.

The other 'Gob Doctors' in Ritchie's CDC (Staff Sergeant Bob Darkin started calling them 'The Dental Maniacs') had a different philosophy about military vehicles though, and they came back to the unit location with a Mercedes Benz lorry they had liberated from a local industrial area. They used it as their personal car and used to drive it at breakneck speed around the units location, much to the disgust of the MTWO (Motor Transport Warrant Officer) of 3 AFA. He tried to curtail their fun by officially taking the vehicle on the units' books and gave it a VRN (Vehicle Registration Number). The Dental Maniacs duly named it Raghead 1 and even Staff Sergeant Bob Darkin made the mistake of going on a mystery tour with them, he thought 'If I can't control them, I might as well keep an eye on them'. On the mystery tour the Dental Driver found a mysterious and massive hole

169

in the desert and he drove the newly acquired German Lorry into it blowing up the vehicles radiator, on inspecting the damage Corporal Moles was scalded by the water from the radiator, much to the other passenger's hilarity. Raghead 1 was 3 AFA's first fatality of the war.

Corporal Mick Killeen RAMC

At Basra International Airport there were two Medical Centres, one British Army, and the other RAF. Mick and his crew were temporarily attached to the army one, the only connection they had with the RAF Medical Centre was to help supply them with medical equipment, of which the RAF seemed to be constantly, in short supply.

The Dining Room of their central feeding cookhouse was in the VIP Lounge of the airport; it also housed an EFI (Expeditionary Forces Institute) shop, which is what the NAAFI is called when deployed on operational tours. It was handy to purchase soft drinks, cigarettes, and sweets. There was also an anteroom with large leather chairs where soldiers of any rank could sit after meals and read a newspaper whilst drinking coffee.

There were the usual rows of tables and chairs in the Dining Room, but on this particular day some of the tables were table clothed with Officers Mess silverware adorning the middle of them. Mick got his scoff and sat down to start eating it when the Commander in Chief (Land Command) Lieutenant General Mike Jackson walked in. He had an entourage of Brigadiers and Colonels fawning over him as he queued up for a meal. The C in C was easily recognised by his maroon beret, gravely voice, and a face that only a mother could love. Mick said to his fellow diners, "Isn't that the bloke we saw on Sky TV news yesterday?"

170

The sycophants attempting to crawl up the Generals arse had prepared the 'Special Table' for the C in C's lunch, they were probably hoping he would be impressed enough to ensure a further step up the promotion ladder. General Jackson looked at the top table and had a look on his face that said, "Nah! Fuck that, I'm going to sit with the lads." He sat at Mick's table and after tucking into the food on his plate he said to the soldier sitting opposite, "Good grub isn't it."

The entourage suddenly started bumping into each other, not sure what to do because the General had thrown a spanner into their beautifully oiled cogs. Mick could almost see the questions that were written over their faces. What should we do? Why is he sitting with the riff raff? Do we now have to sit with the riff raff?

The General had amused Mick.

Captain Sharon Anthony QARANC

The Collecting Sections were still receiving trauma casualties, in one particular case a British soldier came in with severe open abdominal injuries and his mate had a foot that was hanging on to his leg by a mere sinew. But these were only a small part of what the medics had to deal with; the majority of their problems were dealing with the results of the oppressive heat and increased amounts of flies and mosquitoes. There wasn't a cooling wind in the built up area they were operating in and with a lack of latrines and hand washing facilities, D&V (Diarrhoea and Vomiting) was rife amongst the British troops. Cases of this had started earlier when the Section was based at the factory but the number of cases had increased ten fold since arriving at the university. Sharon tasked one of the Armoured Section RAMC Corporal's to set up an isolation ward in the furthest classroom away from everyone else, this was to cut down on the risk of cross contamination. He indignantly stated, "I don't do Primary Care, I only deal with trauma! You're a nurse so you should have to deal with that sort of thing!" Sharon firmly put him in the picture, "Primary Care is the main work load for everyone in this Section at the moment, and we need an isolation ward for all these sick patients, now go and get on with it!" She went to see the Corporal and his patient's a couple of hours later to see how they were all getting on, when she saw the isolation ward she muttered under her breath, "My God." In the classroom the sick patient's had been told to grab any spare floor space they could find. Some were without pillows; blankets and a couple of them didn't even have stretchers and were just lying on the floor. They also only had two bottles of water to be shared between all the patients. The RAMC Corporal medic had made no effort what so ever for his patients and clearly wasn't interested in their welfare.

Sharon took the medic Corporal outside the ward and gave him the bad news, an RAMC Private, also from the Armoured Section, overheard the conversation and said to Sharon, "Leave it to me Ma'am, what exactly do you want doing."
She gave him the following directives:
1. Hand washing facilities set up outside the room.
2. Chemical mats at the room entrance.
3. Every patient must have a stretcher and bedding.
4. All patients must have their own bottled water supply.
5. A chart for each patient to record TPR's (Temperature, Pulse, and Respiration), BP's (Blood Pressure), and any administered drugs.

6. All observations to be carried out and recorded hourly.
7. A medic must be on duty in the ward at all times.
8. A separate latrine organised for these particular patients.

Sharon went back an hour later and the diligent Private had sorted everything and the ward was up and running properly. The patients' diarrhoea and vomiting was treated with Imodium and Maxalon tablets. If they became severely dehydrated they could have an IV put into a vein in their arm, but this was a last resort as puncturing a vein in that environment could lead to the cannulated area getting infected. All the patients in the isolation ward were encouraged to drink as much water as possible and ingest nothing until the diarrhoea had stopped. When they felt well enough to eat they were fed on dry biscuits, and soups from the extra ration packs delivered by the Quartermaster Department. Each of the medics in the unit did a two-hour stag in the Primary Care Ward and Craig the RMO and Sharon did ward rounds every now and again. Most patients were RTU'd (Returned To Unit) within 12 to 24 hours.

Lance Corporal Matt Fairclough RAMC

Matt smoked roll up cigarettes whilst back in the UK because it was cheaper than normal fags and he could stretch out a small pack of tobacco when he was running out of money. But out in Iraq he noticed that his tobacco dried out no matter how he stored it, even tightly wrapped up in a plastic wrapper, and then sealed in a tin container; the tobacco dried out in the incredible heat of the Iraqi desert even before the sealed packaging was opened. He tried putting a piece of potato or fruit skin in the tin with the tobacco to keep it moist but nothing worked. It was like trying to roll up sand in a fag paper. He gave up trying to smoke roll up fags because of this; well, that and the fact he could buy a carton of two hundred Benson and Hedges cigarettes for £3.50 pence from the EFI (Expeditionary Forces Institute).

Sergeant Ritchie John RADC

Soldiers of the British Army can be cruel at times. One of Ritchie's CDC team was a young married man and he hadn't been getting any mail from his wife; he thought she was having an affair with another soldier in Germany whilst he was stuck out in Iraq. He got very depressed about it and his fears were compounded when one of the other lads said, "I bet she is getting a decent portion from some bloke or other, she's probably having a whale of a time while you are tossing it off out here." You can always find sympathy in the British Army; but it is usually in the unit dictionary between the words Shit and Syphilis.

Mail was getting through though as Ritchie found out one night. He had moved into a 9x9 tent and was sharing it with one other soldier who was an RAMC Corporal; the Corporal came into the tent whilst Ritchie was trying to get to sleep. Ritchie was in a bit of a mood and didn't want another meaningless conversation with yet another squaddie fuckwit, so he pretended to be asleep when the Corporal whispered, "Ritchie? Are you awake …Ritchie, can you hear me mate?" When he didn't get any response the Corporal assumed Ritchie was sound asleep and got into his sleeping bag, he then opened his mail which included a jiffy bag in which his wife had sent him a pair of her knickers, after placing them on his head he started to moan and groan as he vigorously masturbated for the next fifteen minutes. Ritchie lay no more than two meters away from him with his fingers in his ears and thinking. 'Oh please God no…'.

<u>Corporal Mick Killeen RAMC</u>

Mick and his crew were on a quiet detachment away from the unit doing medical cover for 3 CS Medical Regiment who were new in theatre and still getting ready to be operational. Mick and Bluey were sunning themselves by their ambulance in the white B&Q garden patio chairs; they were wearing nothing but boxer shorts and knotted handkerchiefs on their heads. The RSM (Regimental Sergeant Major) from 3 CS Medical Regiment pulled up in a Land Rover and came over to talk to them, he was wearing an Australian style bush hat on his head.

Neither of them registered his arrival by jumping to attention because they were busy trying to improve their suntans. Asserting his authority he barked at Bluey "Who are you?" Bluey replied, "I'm Bluey, this is Killer and Mick Pallister is in the back of the Ambulance." Mick got out of his chair and started to walk round the back of the vehicle to give 'Pally' a shout. Incensed by the crew's slovenly and casual manner, the RSM screamed, "DO YOU KNOW WHO I AM?" Bluey turned to Mick and said "Hey Mick! Do you recognise this bloke? He seems to have forgotten who he is." A bollocking and threats ensued before Bluey said to the RSM, "What are you going to do to us? We are TA volunteers stuck out in the middle of the Iraq desert, what the fuck can you possibly do to make our lives any worse than it is today? Send us home? Fucking bring it on sunshine because I've had a gutful of this shit!" Unfortunately for the RSM of 3 CS Medical Regiment, Mick, Bluey, and Pally were becoming rebellious. The RSM went back to his unit Command Post and contacted 1

CS Medical Regiment and had Mick's crew replaced, with Regular Army medics who would give a shit when he shouted at them.

Captain Sharon Anthony QARANC

Diarrhoea and vomiting wasn't the only problem that was decreasing the medical fitness of British troops in Iraq, mosquito bites were playing havoc with just about everyone and if the bites were scratched with dirty fingernails then they usually became infected. Craig, the RMO, had noticed that some of the troops he was seeing were suffering more than others and he started asking which blood group they were as he treated them with anti-histamines and calamine lotion, in severe cases he gave injections of hydrocortisone. Craig and Sharon got to the point where they could identify a patient's blood group as soon as they walked into the Section, those that were badly bitten were blood type A, and those with blood type O were also bitten, but to a far lesser degree. Craig came to the conclusion that soldiers with blood type A must give off some sort of pheromone that attracted mosquitos.

One of Sharon's young female medics was blood type A and she was covered in bites from head to toe, no insect repellent of any kind would stop the plague of little bastards from biting and making her life a misery. Sharon says, "Craig and I thought about evacuating her because she was so badly bitten but whether it was working on patients or doing a stag on the radio, she never wavered from her duties, not even for a minute."

176

Sergeant Ritchie John RADC

Dr Hugh Owen Thomas MRCS invented the Thomas splint in the mid to late 1800's; his nephew Sir Robert Jones was instrumental in improving the design and implementing its use on British Army casualties in the First World War. The splint is made up of a padded ring that surrounds the top of the thigh and hip of a human lower limb, two rigid iron rods extend down from the ring on the inside and outside of the injured leg and are connected by a cross bar at the foot-end. There are numerous accessories that make up the complete set of equipment that is designed to treat casualties with fractured femurs, tibias, fibulas, and those with massive trauma to a lower limb. The splint can only be used with the casualty lying on a stretcher, and after the whole apparatus is set up the casualty's fractured leg can be positioned correctly with the right amount of tension. As long as he has the brains of an Archbishop and a Degree in Engineering, a trained medic can usually complete the setting up task of a Thomas Splint within an hour.

From the start of the First World War and right up to the first Gulf war; all RAMC Field Ambulances deploying on Exercises and Military Operations have taken an abundance of Thomas splints with them, but only a miniscule amount of them have ever been used for real in recent years. All CMT's are taught in how to set up a Thomas splint during their medical training; but once trained; if they don't frequently practice using it they can soon forget how to use this quite complicated piece of medical equipment.

One man who was a champion of the Thomas Splint and an expert on its use was Commander Med; as an RAMC full Colonel from the PFA (Parachute Field Ambulance) he was a link between all British medical units and the Generals at the Coalition Headquarters. On his visit to Ritchie's unit the Medical VIP demanded that the CMT's of 3 AFA give him a demonstration of their skills with the Thomas Splint in front of all the other unit members. This gave Ritchie and Staff Sergeant Bob Darkin a bit of a problem because they had buried 3 AFA's allocation of forty Thomas Splints somewhere in the middle of the Saudi Desert, along with the Chief Clerks U/S photocopying machine. Whilst the CO (Commanding Officer) and his subordinate officers of 3 AFA entertained the Commander of all the Army Medical Services deployed out in Iraq, Ritchie and Bob were tearing around every vehicle in their location and searching the backs of them in the hope that someone, somewhere, had accidentally retained a Thomas Splint. They were in luck and found one buried under some vehicle tarpaulin sheets in the back of a 4 tonner, and they got even luckier as it also had all the accessories needed for the demonstration. After one of Bob's CMT's did a rather successful and impressive show for the visiting bigwig; the last surviving Thomas Splint of 3 AFA was retained in the unit, just in case the RAMC museum back in Aldershot wanted it.

Corporal Mick Killeen RAMC

Another pair of 1 CS Medical Regiment ambulances were parked up outside a Basra civilian hospital, whenever Mick saw other ambulances he would always pulled over to see if they needed any help. The two-story hospital looked like a UK hospital that had been built in the 1960's, the entrance floor was covered in sand and the paint was flaking off the walls. There didn't seem to be much in the way of medical equipment or stores anywhere in the reception area and the patient trolley's seemed to be smeared with some dark sticky substance. The place was filthy.

A female medic was holding a baby and trying to explain to a white-coated Iraqi civilian doctor what was wrong with the parentless infant. The disinterested doctor ordered her to "Put it on the floor over there." The medic continued to try and explain what was wrong with the seriously ill baby and implored the doctor to do an examination and give some treatment. She was getting no joy with the doctor and again she verbally pushed him, "What are you going to do for this child." His reply seemed cold and brusque, "Nothing, not until someone comes up with some money to pay for its care." The female British Army medic was now getting angry and shouted, "Stuff this! We are going to take this baby back to the field ambulance!" The Crew Commander stepped in and said, "No we aren't! We have orders to hand the patient over to the Iraqi Civilian Medical Authorities, and that is what we have to do!" The female medic started crying and became hysterical when the baby she seemed to have bonded with, was taken off her and handed over. As she was bodily removed from the hospital by her crew partners she started screaming, "You can all fuck off, I'm taking that baby back to our lot." She was outnumbered and forced into the ambulance for the drive back to HQ 1 CS Medical Regiment. The baby was left lying on the dirty floor.

Captain Sharon Anthony QARANC

After four or five days of being located at the university, Padre Ian Richardson came to see Sharon and gave her a little present, it was a US Army field shower kit. The kit consisted of a big plastic bag that could hold about 4 litres of water and the bag had a black solar panel moulded onto it, the kit also included a hose, shower head, control valve and a handy little hook to hang the whole contraption up. After filling the bag with water Sharon hung the bag out in direct

179

sunlight and the solar panel heated the water up within fifteen minutes. Sharon hung the shower unit from a hook in the ceiling of a deserted room that had frosted windows still intact; she stood in a large stainless steel bowl and delighted in the absolute bliss of her first shower since leaving England. The water only lasted about ten minutes but for Sharon it felt like the best shower she'd ever had.

Sergeant Ritchie John RADC

Since the war had ended Ritchie's team was being utilised for other routine duties; and this sometimes meant them going on detachments to other units. Lance Corporal Steve Mercer RADC was sent on one of these detachments for a couple of days and was concerned about his 'farm animals', they would need someone to look after them and make sure they were regularly fed. He rather stupidly approached an unsympathetic and very busy Staff Sergeant Bob Darkin with his dilemma and asked if he would look after them for him, "Staff? You just need to pop in now and again to make sure they are alright and feed them maybe once a day." Bob started to think that Steve was clinically insane; but just to get rid of him he agreed to look in on his 'farm' every now and then during his absence from 3 AFA.

When Steve returned to 3 AFA after his detachment; the first thing he did was go to his tent to check on his livestock. The two lizards were lying on their backs with quiet obviously bloated stomachs; they were alive but clearly unwell. Steve went to see Bob and asked what he had done to his precious lizards, Bob told him he hadn't done anything to them except feed them. When he asked Bob what he had been feeding the lizards, Bob honestly told him, "Jaffa Cakes!" Steve shouted, "JAFFA CAKES! But lizards don't like Jaffa Cakes!" Bob sarcastically told Steve,

"I think you will find that they do like Jaffa Cakes because they've fucking well eaten them." On closer inspection of the lizards, Steve could see their mouths were covered in chocolate, and they did seem to be smiling.

Corporal Mick Killeen RAMC

Mick had gone through the entire war wearing European style green and brown coloured DPM (Disruptive Pattern Material) combat clothing. There were not enough Bush Hats to go around either; anyway, those that became available automatically went straight to the Regular Army lads within the unit. Mick says, "All the TA lads were the last to receive any kit that became available, I suppose that was inevitable, if the boot was on the other foot the TA would have done exactly the same."

Desert combats, or 'Dezzies' as they were to become known as, at this stage had become available in all sizes and the RQMS of 1 CS Medical Regiment was trying to issue them out to everyone, including the TA lads. The lads would still have to carry around their old green combats with them; they would be required on return to the UK to 250 in Hull. Mick found out the issue of Desert Combats was purely and simply for the uniformity of the unit photograph that was about to be taken. It would look 'odd' if some of the unit were in green DPM and others were in Dezzies. Mick remembers "I had gone through the war in green, why would I want bloody Dezzies now. I had got that far looking 'odd'; I was going to carry on looking 'odd'. Mick thanked the RQMS but refused the extra kit and looked 'odd' in the photo.

Captain Sharon Anthony QARANC

On the day they arrived at the university it was getting towards dusk by the time they had set up the Section ready to receive any casualties, and as things were quiet, those not on essential duties were organising their sleeping accommodation. The whole Section was accommodated in one of the classrooms and as Sharon sorted her kit out she realised that she had left her doss bag in the back of the Section Soft Top Land Rover. She went outside to get the damn thing before it became to dark to find it. Standing at the back of her Land Rover Sharon could see the sleeping bag up near the front of the vehicle and was about to get in the back to retrieve it when all hell broke loose. The noise of gunfire within the immediate vicinity made her jump out of her skin and dive head first into the back of the Rover, "I've never moved so fast in all my life." admits Sharon. "It was very frightening to be on my own and hear all that gunfire going off all around me. I hadn't got a clue what was going on."

Sharon lay face down in the back of the Rover in a position that is reminiscent of a baby falling asleep on a sofa; she became very conscious of the fact that her bum was sticking up in the air. Her husband Mick's voice popped into her head saying, "Big target love, they won't miss that." She stayed put for about ten minutes until the firing had died down and then dashed back into the building and headed straight for the latrine. Sharon concedes that she is a typical woman; even in the middle of a firefight she still needed to go for a pee.

Lance Corporal Matt Fairclough RAMC

Injuries like heat stroke and heat exhaustion have plagued the British Army since its formation; macho stupidity (Royal Navy Diving Courses included), personal negligence, and just plain old bad management cause most of these types of casualty. When working in severe heat drinking plenty of water and taking extra salt in the diet is essential or the human body will dehydrate very quickly and even the fittest soldier could die. It wasn't any different in Iraq. Matt and his crew collected a casualty suffering from heat stroke from an RAP (Regimental Aid Post) and were tasked to take him to a newly deployed British Field Hospital several miles away. The casualty was in a bad way and despite receiving fluids through an intravenous infusion he was still unconscious and his body temperature was dangerously high. The route to the hospital was on a tarmac road that in the UK would be designated a type of by-pass; there were two lanes on each side of the carriageway. Matt had the blue lights on the top of his ambulance switched on and flashing so that any coalition military vehicles ahead of him would realise he had an emergency case on board and would give him priority and get out of the way. There wasn't too much traffic on the road but ahead of the ambulance in the fast lane was a US Army Hummer vehicle and Matt tailgated it and flashed his headlights to get it to move over and let him past, but it wouldn't give way and Matt had to pass him on the inside lane. As he shot past and continued on his urgent journey Matt saw the passenger side US soldier give him a defiant one-fingered salute.

On arrival at the Field Hospital Matt could see the Doctors, Nurses, and Medics of the new unit all on parade listening to an opening ceremony speech being given by their CO (Commanding Officer). Matt screamed up to the Reception area at break neck speed and the parading troops bomb burst in all directions to avoid getting run over. The Lieutenant Colonel CO came up to Matt's vehicle window and said, "Fantastic timing, we've just opened for business, great to see you." As the casualty was stretchered into the Hospital Reception; Matt saw the US Army Hummer vehicle that blocked his passage on the way in, also pull into the Field Hospital, it passed Matt's ambulance and parked about twenty meters away. Matt approached an American MP (Military Policeman) who was involved in guarding the compound and told him not only of the delay that particular vehicle had caused him, but the fact that its passenger had also given him the bird. The MP chuckled and said, "That's not an insult, it's the way we say hello in the states." Matt was still fuming at the incident on the road and told the MP, "I wasn't fucking born yesterday, and you had better go and tell that ugly wanker that when a British army Ambulance has its blue lights flashing they should get out of the fucking way!" The MP apologised and went over to remonstrate with the American occupants of the Hummer vehicle, Matt could see him making a masturbating hand gesture to the occupant and then pointed over towards where Matt was standing, he then came back with a big grin on his face. "The female 2nd Lootenant sends her apologies, she didn't realise you had a casualty on board!" Matt walked into the hospital muttering "Stupid fucking cow."

Sergeant Ritchie John RADC

Ritchie attended yet another O Group; but this one was held in the OC's tent. The Major was obviously enjoying the importance of the occasion, he solemnly turned to his troops and said, "From 1200 hours tomorrow morning all hostilities will cease between the Coalition and Iraqi Forces, gentlemen, the war is over." Ritchie turned to Bob and said,

"Fuck me that was quick. It's a bit like hiring a prostitute, all that money and it's over and done with, what a waste of fucking money!"

Corporal Mick Killeen RAMC

Richard Branson flew into Basra International Airport on one of his Virgin Airways 747s; this massive aircraft was the first civilian airliner to land in Iraq since the war had ended. There was a mass of soldiers, officers, civilians and dignitaries to welcome him under the gaze of the world's media. The plane was carrying humanitarian aid for the Iraqi people, though Mick wondered how useful the baby incubators would be because Basra didn't have any electrical power. A set of mobile steps was driven up to the 747 as the front cabin door was opened and out stepped a long legged blonde cabin crewmember. She posed on the top step as soldiers from the Black Watch and Parachute Regiment started shouting, "Show us your legs," she raised her skirt and flashed her beautiful pins. Encouraged by this, they then started shouting, "Show us your fur burger," but sadly for all the soldiers present she couldn't hear their second request. Richard Branson walked down the steps and was greeted by a crowd of reporters and army officers, all to the sound of a thousand cameras clicking.

At the rear of the plane the cargo doors, which were 30 meters above the ground, had been opened to unload all the humanitarian stores. Large hydraulic lifts were raised and lowered to unload the kit and then handed over to the waiting forklift drivers. An RAF Clerk was ordered onto the lift to help unload because it was to be a quick turn around for the aircraft, everyone available had to help. The Clerk pointed out, "I'm a Clerk, what the fuck do I know about unloading aircraft." He was told, "It's only humping and dumping, just get on with it," and that is exactly what he did, but under protest. Unfortunately he fell off the lift when it was at its maximum height and hit every bit of metalwork on the way down.

Meanwhile back at the ranch, Mick was enjoying the Branson/Media show until someone came running up to his ambulance shouting, "We've got a casualty at the rear of the plane, and he's a Priority One so get over there quickly!" An RAMC Corporal medic called Jasmine grabbed her Crash Bag and doubled over to where the incident was unfolding whilst Mick, Palley and Bluey got into the Ambulance and drove over. The casualty was screaming his head off when they arrived at the scene, Palley cut away his trousers so he could examine his injuries and saw the clerk had deformity in his lower legs due to fractures of both sets of Tibia and Fibula's. Mick could see the ends of the bones trying to break through the skin.

A member of an RAF Puma helicopter aircrew suddenly appeared at the incident and shouted "We've got a chopper up and running to evacuate him if you need us, it's a three minute flight to the Field Hospital." By this stage Palley had gently straightened the casualty's legs and immobilised them with splints, padding and a figure of eight bandage around his ankles. A female doctor from 1 CS started to take over and shouted, "Take his fucking boots off, I need to check his circulation is alright." Mick said, "Ma'am! We've got a chopper up and running to get him straight to the hospital, he will be in a treatment bay in less than four minutes!" She was not going to listen to a jumped up medic and insisted that his boots be removed, the support to his legs were taken off and the casualty screamed even louder as he went through the agony of the doctor unsuccessfully trying to take his boots off. Turning to Jasmine she shouted, "I need 10

Mils of morphine, get it drawn up for me now." Jasmine did as instructed and presented the syringe and needle whilst showing the bottle it had been drawn up from, this is always done so the person injecting can confirm the drug and make sure it is in date. The doctor grabbed the bottle, threw it across the runway and screamed, "That's no fucking good, it's out of date!" Jasmine grabbed her own Bergen and drew up the required morphine from an in date bottle that she carried. The doctor injected the morphine but instead of promptly evacuating the casualty she decided on doing a secondary examination, someone shouted, "For fucks sake Ma'am, there's a chopper waiting, get him on the aircraft and check him out on route, lets get this poor fucker on his way to hospital!" An RAF non-medical female officer was trying to comfort him by squeezing and patting his left arm, the arm was also fractured and caused him to cry out because of the pain she was inflicting.

Eventually the doctor allowed the casualty to be loaded on the Puma and he was belatedly flown to the Field Hospital. When everything had calmed down the doctor turned on Jasmine and said, "Don't you ever give me out of date drugs to be administered to a patient." Jasmine retaliated, "The morphine came out of your fucking treatment Bergen, Ma'am! The in date drug came out of my Bergen." The doctor was not going to accept part of the responsibility, "Yes! Well that's not the point, you should have checked!" Jasmine had the final word, "If your personal admin was on the ball, we wouldn't be having this conversation...Ma'am."

Richard Branson and the reception committee were totally unaware of what had happened at the rear of the 747 but when put in the picture at a later date, he apparently offered a free holiday to the RAF Clerk and his family when he was fully recovered.

Captain Sharon Anthony QARANC

A 432-tracked armoured ambulance from the SDG's was tasked to give medical cover for a mission at bridge 4 and it was Sharon's turn to provide the medical expertise as a crewmember. They were parked up near the bridge on stand by just in case the Infantry or Tankies suffered any casualties during the fighting. A large and hostile Iraqi crowd had gathered near the bridge and Sharon could hear a 'ping ping ping' sound on the outside of the ambulance. She looked up at the Crew Commander and said, "For God's sake, can't they see the bloody red crosses on the vehicle, why are they throwing rocks at us, we're medics!" The Crew Commander looked down at Sharon, tutted, and said in a patronising voice, "Those aren't rocks Ma'am, they are bullets."

The firing intensified to such a level that the Crew Commander decided the ambulance had to be moved clear of the area before the ambulance crew themselves became casualties. He shouted at the driver through the intercom system, "GO! GO! GO!" Another TA soldier in the back of the ambulance was providing protection at the rear door and thought the Crew Commander was shouting at him, he leapt into action, opened the door and jumped out to engage the enemy. As the rounds hit the ground by his feet and the 432 started to move off he instinctively leapt back into the ambulance in one swift movement and shouted, "Oh Shit!"

Lance Corporal Matt Fairclough RAMC

The British Army Medical Services in Iraq had an abundance of CMT's but there was a shortage of Drivers for their ambulances, so the less experienced and qualified

CMT's, which included Matt, changed roles and became Drivers to make up for the shortfall.

One night when Matt and his Crew were resting outside an RAP at the old Basra Airport they were given a 'shout' to go to a nearby Field Hospital, the hospital was only about five minutes drive away. As the Crew were on 'Immediate' standby they had to remain fully booted and suited, they were on a sixty second notice to move. Matt drove at speed to the Reception area and parked at the hospital entrance. The Crew Commander was surprised when told to "Wait Out as the casualty wasn't stable enough to be moved yet, this is purely a patient transfer task, when the patient is stabilised you will have to transport him to an Iraqi civilian hospital in Basra." The other Crew Members wandered off to see if they could scrounge some cold drinks and left Matt and Fred, who was the RLC Driver of the other ambulance, smoking and drinking tea as they waited by their ambulances. All RLC ambulance drivers wear a Red Cross armband but can only be differentiated from RAMC medics by the fact that the Red Cross is slightly smaller. The doctor who was treating the casualty they had come to pick up was a TA Major, he said, "Ah medics, you don't often get to see this sort of stuff, why don't you come in and have a look." Matt and Fred followed the Major into the operating theatre and they noticed an unconscious Iraqi civilian lying on his back with an airway inserted into what was left of his mouth. The majority of his lower jaw and teeth on the left hand side of his head had been ripped off; he also had shrapnel wounds to his forehead and scalp. Through the skill of the British Surgeons they had managed to save both his legs even though a lot of the muscle had been torn off the lower parts of the limbs.

The Major explained that the 30 year old Iraqis' donkey had stood on an anti-personnel mine, the donkey had absorbed most of the blast and had bizarrely saved the mans life while nearly taking it at the same time. Matt bizarrely asked, "What happened to the donkey?" Fred started to turn green at the sight of the casualty's injuries and said, "I've had enough of this, I'm going outside." Matt explained to the Major that Fred was an RLC driver and not a medic, and therefore not really into the surgical side of army life. The ambulance crews would have to wait around for about forty minutes before they could move this casualty and finish the job.

Sergeant Ritchie John RADC

The war was over and Ritchie was looking forward to getting back to Osnabruck, he desperately needed beer and the company of members of the opposite sex. He also needed to get his discharge from the British Army initiated, the sooner he became a civilian and distanced himself from the moronic officers he had served under, the better he would feel. But it would be six weeks before Ritchie and 3 AFA got their turn to go home, and before that time came the OC of 3 AFA had some ideas on how to keep everyone occupied. The men were bored senseless during the war phase and now hostilities had ceased; they just seemed to be hanging around with even less to do, at one stage the OC had the unit doing litter sweeps in the desert. Any soldiers not on duty had to form an extended line and walk across the desert picking up any discarded cigarette butts and waste paper. The problem with bored restless soldiers is that they can be a dangerous and volatile entity. The best thing to do as far as the OC was concerned was to keep the men busy and so he ordered a unit move, all 3 AFA's tentage and equipment was packed up onto the unit vehicles and they all

190

headed off to a new location with the OC leading the way in his Land Rover.

For the next twenty-four hours Ritchie and his 'Gob Doctors' were bounced around the back of a 4 Tonner that was overloaded with stretchers and other medical paraphernalia. The rough ground the convoy drove over made it impossible to do anything other than hang on for dear life; it was a relief when the OC occasionally stopped the convoy so the men could have a comfort stop to stretch their legs and have a piss.

When the convoy pulled up at the units new desert location everyone got out of the vehicles and started setting up all the tents and equipment. Ritchie became apoplectic with rage as he looked around him and realised they were in exactly the same place they had left twenty-four hours earlier.

Corporal Mick Killeen RAMC

All ammunition had to be handed in to the RQMS of 5 GS Medical Regiment before the TA lads were formally transferred over to 1 CS. An official parade was organised for all of the transferring soldiers to hand in their ammo and receive new ammo from 1CS. Mick was bewildered with the units' idiotic and senseless bureaucracy, they could just as well have kept the same ammo they were issued when they arrived in theatre. It is decreed a heinous crime in the British Army for a soldier to lose his weapon or any of his ammunition, it could be picked up and used by the enemy to kill or maim soldiers from his own side. The RQMS had a wooden tray that measured exactly one hundred rounds at a time, but Mick knew he was missing six rounds.

Mick had visions of a Court Martial finding him guilty, locking him up in the Military Prison in Colchester and throwing away the key. At the time Mick said "Of all the thousands of rounds of ammunition I have handed in throughout this fucking war, why didn't I keep some back just in case?" Hindsight is such a useless gift.

Bluey came into the back of the ambulance where Mick had counted out his ammo, "Never mind Killer, take what you need out of this lot." He then dumped a hessian sandbag full of British Army 5.56mm ammunition. Mick could have kissed him.

Captain Sharon Anthony QARANC

On Sharon's second night at the university she noticed how the temperature was getting hotter and hotter, it got to the stage where everyone was sleeping in his or her sleeping bag liners and just lying on top of the doss bags. The Section was sharing the accommodation with Captain Towart who was the Scots Dragoon Guards' Motor Transport Officer and an experienced ex ranker soldier, because of the heat he slept in only his boxer shorts. They were all abruptly shaken out of their sleep by the sound of gunfire in the corridor outside their accommodation and someone started shouting "STAND TO! STAND TO!" This is the signal that let's soldiers know their location is under attack and they must spring into action to defend themselves, their comrades and their location. In the case of medics they must also fight to protect their patients. The attack was due to some Iraqi soldiers assaulting the prisoner compound and attempting to release their comrades.

Sharon jumped out of her sleeping bag liner, cocked her pistol and thought for the first time in her life that she may have to actually shoot someone, she openly admits, "Because of the sheer volume of noise from the gunfire in the building it really was quite frightening." Captain Towart was the first one up and ready to react, he cocked his SA 80 rifle and knelt by the door wearing just his boxer shorts and army helmet, "I've got it covered," he shouted. In the stress of the moment Sharon giggled and thought, 'I hope he's got everything else covered as well.' She also did a head count of all her soldiers and found only one was unaccounted for, her Section Sergeant. He was cowering behind the Section fridge that had been placed in the room to stop other units trying to nick it. He hadn't got his personal weapon in his hands and he also gave no orders or reassurance to the young 18-year-old soldiers in his Section, he in effect abandoned them to fend for himself. Sharon was seething with anger about his timid display during the firefight, which is when historically, British SNCO's, stand up, and are counted.

Talk of his faint-hearted display spread around the unit very quickly and the story went that he was actually trying to hide inside the fridge itself.

Lance Corporal Matt Fairclough RAMC

Matt was really impressed by the TA doctor who was dealing with the man injured when his donkey had stood on a mine; the RAMC Major had no airs or graces at all and spoke to Matt as if he were an old acquaintance. They both chatted for the next forty minutes until the casualty was stable enough to be moved to an Iraqi Civilian Hospital, Fred drove the lead ambulance and Matt moved the still unconscious casualty into the back of his vehicle. Pete sat in the front with Matt whilst Carol travelled in the back of the ambulance with no less than, the casualty, the RAMC doctor, an anaesthetist, a QARANC nurse and finally, crammed in the corner, was the injured man's mother. Matt describes the procession as "A fucking Charabanc outing." The casualty's life signs were constantly checked with a sphygmomanometer (monitors Blood Pressure), ECG (Heart Monitor), and a Pulse oximeter (Blood Oxygen levels).

The ambulances travelled slowly through the streets of Basra and when they finally arrived at the local hospital, the RAMC doctor and QARANC nurse got out the back of the ambulance to speak to the Iraqi hospital staff prior to handing over the casualty. When the Iraqi medics saw the state of the casualty's face, the hospital doctor said, "Not here, we can not deal with any Maxilla Facial injuries, you must take him to the University Hospital." Matt asked a question, "Does anyone from our lot know where that is?" An English speaking Iraqi doctor volunteered to show Matt the way to the hospital and sat in the front of the ambulance, Pete joined Carol and the others in the now severely overcrowded rear of the ambulance. Just before Matt drove off, a car came screeching up to the front of the hospital and unceremoniously dumped a body onto the ground. Two hospital porters came out with a rickety old gurney, they picked up the body and threw it on the trolley and took him inside the building, and the Iraqi doctor turned to Matt and ironically said, "This is our ambulance drop off point." He then gave instructions on how to get to the University Hospital, "At the end of the road we need to turn left." This was turning out to be the most protracted job Matt had been on since deploying, and it wasn't over yet.

Sergeant Ritchie John RADC

In wartime, women like to write to soldiers as pen pals in the belief they are helping to keep up the troops morale, that and the fact that the female of the species are known to be turned on by men they think have killed for their country. Any young ladies who wrote to a soldier who deployed out on the first Gulf War might want to skip this anecdote.

The lads of 3 AFA hunted through mail sacks holding thousands of battered envelopes addressed to 'A soldier in the Gulf', some times they were addressed more specifically to 'A medic in the Gulf'. Some of these letters were written by men and were addressed to 'A Nurse in the Gulf' and the lads thought they were from either a pervert or some sort of social leper who just wanted to get into the knickers of a QARANC nurse. The letters from women were eagerly accepted though because they usually enclosed a photograph of themselves, and believe it or not some of them sent pictures of themselves in a naked and seductive pose that could be masturbated over. The lads also thought these women might be desperate for a good shag and if they were not bad looking, they would be worth visiting after getting back from the Gulf. In 3 AFA's Reception area, some plywood British Army Figure Eleven rifle targets were erected and transformed into a 'Gallery of Operation Granby Growlers'. The photos were placed on the board in priority of ugliness, the more repulsive the woman was deemed to be, the higher up the pecking order she was placed.

Corporal Chris Scard was on duty one night and found a particular letter from a 17-year-old young lad who had addressed it to 'A nurse in the Gulf'. For a bit of a laugh Chris decided to reply to the young lad and introduced himself as Christine, letters were sent between the two of them over the coming weeks, the letters were compiled by Chris and with the help of other sexual deviants like Ritchie and Bob Darkin, the letters became more and more sexually explicit. In the end the young 17-year old lad was looking forward to a Gulf War Victory weekend in London with Christine and all the sexual pleasures any teenager could possibly envisage. The lad then made the mistake of asking for a photograph of Christine so he would recognise her when they eventually met up; a battered Polaroid picture was duly dispatched to the young lad. The picture showed about fifteen medics and RCT drivers with blackened faces and their knobs hanging out, the accompanying letter explained that these were in fact the blokes he had been writing to and expressing his undying love. The last letter remains unanswered to this very day and no one knows exactly how traumatised the young lad is as a result of his dreadful literary experience with 3 AFA.

Corporal Mick Killeen RAMC

There wasn't much to buy in Iraq as food and accommodation was taken care of by the Ministry of Defence, so the majority of British soldiers only drew about 50 US Dollars (All allied currency in Iraq was in US Dollars) from their pay. The average cost of 200 Benson and Hedges cigarettes was 7 US Dollars, about £3.50 pence. Mick spent most of his fortnightly pay on smoking up to 80 cigarettes a day, pot noodles, Pringles and silly T-shirts embossed with unit logos. All the Hull lads were going home soon, and Mick decided to splash the cash and get a great present to take home to Jean.

In the lobby of the Shat El Arab hotel in Basra Mick saw an Iraqi man standing behind a stall, he was wearing a Dish Dash (Long robe) and was selling rugs, trinkets, lighters and various other gaudy items. It was apparently like a scene out of the film Casablanca, the only thing missing was Humphrey Bogart standing underneath the spinning ceiling fan. On the stall Mick spotted a lime green coloured alarm clock in the shape of a mosque. It was made out of plastic, had gold plastic edging and when the alarm went off, it played all seventeen verses of the Koran calling Muslims' to prayer. A white light that could destroy an average retina brightly shone out as the wailing started. Mick thought, 'Now that is class, I'm sure Jean will love it'. It wasn't and Jean didn't. "How much for the clock" asked Mick? The Iraqi salesman gave an opening offer of 5 US Dollars. Mick started to haggle, "No mate, it's got to be worth a lot more than that, this is for my wife, I don't want to buy any cheap tat, I'll give you 10 US Dollars." The Iraqi was confused, he was supposed to be haggled to lower the price, not raise it, Mick managed to negotiate the price up to 15 US Dollars.

Mick walked back to his ambulance clutching Jean's God awful present and left the Iraqi scratching and shaking his head whilst looking at the pile of money in his hand.

Captain Sharon Anthony QARANC

Because of the attack at the prisoner compound all the medical units were moved back to the airfield, Sharon was immediately conscious of how much cooler it was outside the urban area of their last location. One week later all the fighting had really quietened down so Sharon and the Padre, Captain Ian Richardson, went to the Field Hospital to visit some of the casualties that had passed through and been treated in their Section. The soldier with the severe open abdominal injuries was still very poorly but his vital signs were improving daily.

After finishing their visits they were leaving the hospital and Sharon spotted some 5 GS ambulances parked up near the entrance, she immediately recognised the faces of the soldiers stood by the vehicles, they were from 250 Field Ambulance. Mick Killeen, Palley Pallister, Bluey, Neil Goodwin and Paul Greenside were shooting the breeze whilst having a brew; Mick was wearing a pair of shorts that Sharon can only describe as "Awful." Sharon ran up to them and started taking the piss immediately; she pointed at Mick's legs and said, "Put those bloody things away will you." "It was like being back at home in Wenlock Barracks as we stood around for the next hour just talking and taking the Mickey out of each other." Sharon was an officer and they were all NCOs, so a certain amount of decorum and protocol should have been maintained, that's how it would have been done in the Regular British Army. But the big difference with these TA soldiers was that they were also friends and so Mick gave Sharon a big hug and for the first time since she had arrived in Iraq, Sharon felt really happy. Being an officer and commanding troops is often a very cold and lonely position at the best of times, but to do it as a TA officer in charge of Regular Army troops who treat you with indifference, is more than a challenge.

Over the next few weeks Sharon made excuse after excuse to go back to the same spot just in the hope of seeing some of her 250 Field Ambulance friends again

Lance Corporal Matt Fairclough RAMC

On the way to the University Hospital Matt drove slowly because the ambulance was overcrowded and the roads in Basra were in such a poor condition, several times he had to shout through the window to the medics in the back, "Big hole in the road! Hang on to something!" It was a long and painfully slow journey getting this severely wounded man into the care of his local hospital.

198

The turning circle of a British Army Ambulance is not dissimilar to that of the ocean liner QE 2, and the approach road to the University Hospital was narrow and had several sharp turns to negotiate. Matt therefore decided to reverse his ambulance down the road so the casualty could be extracted straight from the rear of the vehicle and up the steps into the hospital, he would also be able to exit the location rapidly and easily if necessary. Fred stood at the front of the ambulance and guided Matt backwards using hand signals to indicate when he should turn the steering wheel, by guiding the ambulance back he was also able to help Matt avoid running down a crowd of women who had gathered at the hospital entrance wailing at the top of their voices. After guiding the ambulance to the base of the steps Fred doubled back up the road to his own ambulance, he left Matt to push his way through the shrieking crowd of Iraqi women to help get the casualty inside the hospital. An Iraqi man stepped forward and started slapping the women around the head and was obviously verbally abusing them so they would make way for Carol, Pete and the other medics to carry out their task. Matt said, "Hang on a minute mate, there's no need for that." Matt gesticulated to the women by waving his hands and saying in a loud enough voice to be heard over their caterwauling, "Could you ladies please move to one side!" Surprisingly they actually gave way but continued with their insufferable vocal histrionics. Everyone in the back of Matt's ambulance helped carry the casualty inside the hospital and left Matt outside to guard the vehicle, he was joined by an old Iraqi man who said to Matt, "Ah! You Jidah." Matt replied, "Yeah I'm a soldier, but a medical one not infantry." The old man asked, "When you go home" to which Matt told him "Soon." The old man went on, "We thank you for what you have done but it is now time for you to leave and go home to your families." The old chap's eyes lit up when Matt took out a packet of

Benson and Hedges cigarettes and fired one up; Matt gave the old man one and received a packet of twenty Iraqi cigarettes in return. Diplomatically Matt returned the favour and gave the old man a couple of packets of his Benson and Hedges fags. The old man said that he liked the English, he pulled out a strip of ICI tablets from his pocket and showed them to Matt, he then pulled off his hat to reveal a severe dent in his head, it was an injury he suffered whilst fighting as a soldier during the Iran/Iraq war. He had apparently been evacuated to the UK for surgery and he considered the English his saviours. The two of them continued talking and waited for the medics to return to the ambulance so Matt could transport them back to their Field Hospital.

Sergeant Ritchie John RADC

Ritchie jumped at the chance to go on a jolly and visit 5 AFA who were one of 3 AFA's sister units, they were located in some other part of the vast wilderness of desert, and Ritchie would be travelling in the back of a 3 AFA soft top Land Rover. Commanding the journey was Staff Sergeant Bob Darkin, and Staff Sergeant Mick Germaine would be driving the vehicle, Mick was the unit CQMS (Company Quarter Master Sergeant) who dealt with all the units' stores and resupply requisitions. They weren't going for a particular reason, it was just a quick trip to get out of the claustrophobic confines of the Dressing Station, with a bit of luck they might get to meet other medic and 'Gob Doctor' friends they hadn't seen since deploying out to Saudi. They had also heard that unlike 3 AFA, 5 AFA had some female medics in their unit and Ritchie was desperate to go and have a lecherous ogle, he hoped that he might even get to fumble one of them. The RCT Drivers knew the area well because they travelled to other units every day, they told Mick it would be easy enough to find 5 AFA's location, he would simply have to drive up the tarmac road until he came across the decapitated Iraqi soldier at the T junction and turn right, he then had to keep going on that road and 5 AFA were located on the left hand side and could be seen from the road itself. Mick first paraded the Land Rover to make sure it was full of diesel and they set off without any further preparations, as they would only be gone for a couple of hours and 5 AFA would provide them with lunch, there was no need to take any water or rations with them.

It was going to take at least a couple of hours to get to 5 AFA and as the directions were so simple none of the jolly boys bothered to take any maps or compasses with them. When they got to the decapitated Iraqi soldier at the T-junction they turned left as the RCT Drivers had told them. There was some discussion between the three of them as to whether or not they should be turning left or right, in the end they convinced each other that turning left felt the right (pardon the pun) thing to do. After driving for another couple of hours they ran out of tarmac road and were driving over firm desert ground with no point of reference anywhere. Of the three, Ritchie was the only one who had brought a water bottle with him and that was about half full. As they drove further and further into the desert Bob had noticed Ritchie's grip on their only water supply was getting tighter and tighter. Bob asked the frightening question that was on all their lips, "Where the fuck are we?" Mick was the first to answer, "I have no fucking idea, but one thing is for sure, we only have just over half of our diesel left and if that runs out we are well and truly fucked." Ritchie tried to hide his water bottle behind his back. They continued driving until Bob spotted something on the horizon; there were some vehicles and tents with a military flag flying above whichever unit it was, they all hoped it was 5 AFA's location. Bob used his binoculars and identified the flag, he was positive it was the national flag of either Iran or Iraq; both the Iranian and Iraqi flags are very similar and Bob openly admits, "My knowledge of flags of the world is very limited." If it was an Iranian flag they would probably be welcomed with open arms, after all, they were British Army and they had just defeated Iran's neighbouring enemies, but if it was an Iraqi flag then the disgruntled and defeated Iraqi's would more than likely want to do them some serious harm.

Discretion was the better part of valour and they beat a hasty retreat and tried to retrace the route that had bought them to the middle of one of the most barren and desolate places on earth. More by sheer luck than soldiering skills, they found the T-junction with the decapitated Iraqi soldier and headed back to 3 AFA's location, by the time they pulled up outside the Dressing Station, Ritchie's water bottle was empty and the Land Rover was running on fumes. There was a very real danger of them running out of fuel, no one knew where they were, and they could well have died of thirst before anyone accidentally found them. Bob turned to Mick and Ritchie and said, "Let us never ever talk about this to anyone, should someone find out what a trio of fucking idiots we really are, I personally will die of embarrassment."

Corporal Mick Killeen RAMC

All the Hull TA lads who were still in Theatre were given three days notice of their impending return to the UK. They were held at a transit camp where personal weapons had to be handed in for conveyance back to the UK in the aircraft cargo bays, no one was allowed to carry personal weapons on board the aircraft. Body armour also had to be handed in for use by replacement troops, of which there seemed to be a constant stream flying into Iraq. The admin staff was also looking for HGV drivers to go back as a sea party and take some vehicles back to Germany. Mick was an HGV 1 driver but kept 'schtum' as a long sea trip to Hamburg would have delayed his family reunion with Jean, Rachel, and Victoria. He just wanted to go home, but if they ordered him to drive an army wagon and go home by sea on a rusty Royal Navy bucket; he would of course...tell them to "Go fuck themselves!" He was lucky, they didn't ask.

At 1600 hours a coach took all returning troops bound for the UK to Basra International Airport in civilian coaches. Mick felt naked and vulnerable without the personal weapon, body armour, and ammunition that he had been carting around for the last six months. The only personal protection he would have on the hour-long coach trip to the airport would be his Kevlar helmet and a coach window curtain to hide behind. The troops weren't going to be totally defenceless though, they were to be escorted by long wheel-based Land Rovers that were brimming with GPMG's (General Purpose Machine Guns) and heavily armed infantrymen. As Mick put his Bergen and webbing into the loading area underneath the coach, he was suddenly reminded of all the TA Summer Camp Endex's (End of Exercise) he had experienced. He expected some one to shout, "The Junior Ranks bar will be open when we get back to Wenlock Barracks but only after all vehicles are unloaded and weapons handed into the armoury."

In the airport lobby all the departing troops formed a queue to wait processing by the Movements Clerks who would check all baggage and documentation. As Mick shuffled forward he saw a large sign that stated,

'NO KNIVES, HANDGUNS, BAYONETS, RIFLES OR AMMUNITION OF ANY KIND ARE PERMITTED TO

BE TAKEN ON YOUR FLIGHT. PLEASE DEPOSIT ANY ILLEGAL ITEMS IN THE BIN PROVIDED'.

A dustbin sized grey cardboard container was sited next to the sign and as Mick drew level with it he noticed it was full of AK 47's, pistols, bayonets, Arabian swords and a vast assortment of ammunition. Mick swears he actually saw a hand grenade in the bin. Soldiers obviously wanted to take these souvenirs back home to the UK, but if they were caught smuggling them onto the plane the penalties were severe. Imprisonment itself would have been bad enough, let alone further separation from loved ones and beer.

Mick had some shrapnel that he wanted to take back to Hull for use in TA lectures to elucidate, to those who hadn't deployed, exactly what sort of things could come flying towards them when the 'shit hits the fan'. A Movements Clerk said to Mick, "Sorry chum, all this sort of stuff has to go in the bin; no sharp objects that can be used as a weapon can be taken on board." Mick understood and dropped the very sharp and heavy metal pieces into the bin but Mick Pallister refused to surrender his Stretcher Bearer Scissors. He pleaded, "I've used these throughout the war on many casualties and they have great sentimental value, I really want to take them home with me." Pally was allowed to keep the scissors on condition they were put in his Bergen, and not carried on board but stored in the aircraft cargo bay.

The baggage x-ray machine operator had noted something in Mick's Bergen and he was called forward to identify it, the mystery object was an 18x12 inch metal information sign that Mick had 'borrowed' from the airport some months earlier. The sign was headed BASRA INTERNATIONAL AIRPORT and said in English and Iraqi italics, 'We thank you for not smoking'. After 'borrowing' it off the wall Mick

204

had used the sign to write all his letters home, and like Pally's scissors, it had sentimental value. The sign had to go in the bin though as the British Army didn't want to offend the Iraqi people by stealing their no smoking signs.

As the Bergen went on a conveyer belt to be loaded on the aircraft Mick swiped his ID card through the Bar Coding machine for the second time, and was officially registered with the MOD as leaving Iraq. Mick sarcastically asked the Movements Clerk "Can I have cash back?" The clerk didn't even crack a smile.

Captain Sharon Anthony QARANC

The Iraqi Army infrastructure had collapsed and the war was over so Sharon, and all the other detached medics with the SDG's and 2 RTR (Royal Tank Regiment) were transferred from their Collecting Sections, back into the hub of 1 CS Medical Regiment who were also based at the airfield. One of the 1 CS officers told Sharon, "You are contracted to this unit for six months so you will be staying here whilst we send some of our Regular officer's home. Sharon was adamant, "No we are not! We are only contracted to the British Army whilst the war is on going, hostilities have ceased, and we should now be sent home to the UK!" Sharon won the argument but it would be weeks before she eventually got on a flight because there were thousands of flights to be arranged for all the returning troops.

I CS soldiers just sat around for weeks doing nothing apart from some Primary Care work as thousands of soldiers were going down with severe bouts of D and V, the medics advised units to stop their troops from communal cooking (They were throwing their rations into one pot, heating the food and all eating from it), and try to get them to improve on their personal hygiene. This was the major factor in causing the epidemic.

The female OC of Sharon's Squadron in 1 CS Medical Regiment spoke to the Squadron personnel to brief them on what was going to happen in the near future, "This unit is now going onto the next phase of our deployment which will be in a peace keeping action and this unit will be used in this phase in a supporting role." Towards the end of her briefing she gave a little speech and said, "At this time we will also be losing some of our attached troops who are returning to the UK, I said at the start of this deployment that I didn't want any TA soldiers in my Squadron, well, I am now going to have to eat a huge slice of humble pie. All the TA soldiers who have served alongside us regulars have done a fantastic job and behaved in a most professional manner, we certainly couldn't have completed our missions without their help. Thank you."

Lance Corporal Matt Fairclough RAMC

After handing the casualty over to the civilian Iraqi medical staff in the University hospital, Carol, Pete, the Major, the anaesthetist and lastly the QARANC nurse all returned to the ambulance where Matt was still waiting. The Major jumped into the front seat of the ambulance quoting "R.H.I.P." meaning, Rank Has It's Privileges. As Matt pulled away from the hospital the Major complimented him on his careful driving and for transporting the casualty to the hospital safely and without any unnecessary drama. He also mentioned that he and the other Field Hospital staff were enjoying this trip because, since arriving in Iraq, none of them had been outside the claustrophobic environment of the Field Hospital location. As a favour Matt offered to take them on a sight seeing tour of Saddam Hussein's palace, which was now the location of Headquarters 1 CS Medical Regiment RAMC, and as it was on the way back to their unit it wasn't much of a detour.

The Major's Field Hospital was the same unit that Matt, 'Murph' and 'Paddy', had taken the casualties that had been severely burnt in the tanker explosion. Matt described the family and their injuries to the Major and asked if he knew what had happened to them, "I was one of the surgeons that treated them when they came into the hospital, you and your crew did a great job, and they certainly survived, they were flown to Cyprus for specialised treatment on their burns." Matt felt a lump in his throat and a huge sense of pride in what he; 'Murph' and 'Paddy' had succeeded in doing.

Sergeant Ritchie John RADC

On their last unit move 3 AFA headed in towards Kuwait City, according to Ritchie's war diary, the six hour journey was, "Bloody awful". He was cramped up in the cab of an MK 4 Tonner and took over some of the driving duties from the RCT Driver to give him a rest; through the vehicle windows he saw thousands of Iraqi Prisoners Of War who were being herded away into captivity. They all looked dirty, tired, hungry and totally dejected, Ritchie was amazed at the prisoners reactions after reaching the POW camp, they seemed to be delighted that the British Army provided them with secure accommodation, a hot meal and a chance to get some proper sleep, something they hadn't had for weeks on end. And although Ritchie felt sorry for these poorly led and equipped Iraqi soldiers, they were luckier than their dead comrades who were scattered at the side of the road, they seemed to have been abandoned by everyone. Eventually soldiers of the Royal Pioneer corps were tasked to collect and deal with all the Iraqi dead.

On arrival at their final location, 3 AFA set up their tents in an industrial area that was on the edge of Kuwait city itself, every building on the industrial estate had been pillaged and plundered by the retreating Iraqi soldiers, what they couldn't steal, they had simply destroyed. Other units were also located with the medics and not far from their location was an airstrip where coalition C 130's and civilian airliners took off and landed all day long. But it would be six long weeks before the 3 AFA medics got their chance to board an airliner and go home to their families in BAOR. To entertain, and keep themselves busy, the medics of 3 AFA set about organising a concert party. A stage was constructed by parking two M K 4 tonners back to back with their tail and side boards dropped, scrim nets were strategically placed around and over the wagons to give the ensemble a theatrical appearance. On a permanent basis, the following items were borrowed from a nearby mosque that had been ravaged by the retreating Iraqi army, some stage-lights, a sound system and some comfy chairs for the audience to sit on. Ritchie was heavily involved in the stage show as he did a black, male, and macho portrayal of Cilla Black for a farcical version of Blind Date, "I was totally in my element and having a great time …the entertainment world…Oh the life." Three male contestants were assembled on the improvised stage that was divided by a Hessian curtain, on the other side of the curtain was Ritchie and the prize of the competition, Private Dee McCarthy who was a very attractive QARANC Dental Nurse. She had been visiting the unit and had been noticed by all the sex-starved medics, Ritchie persuaded Dee to take part in the show, the medics put two and two together and realised a date with her was the prize. She asked several inane questions to the three medics and then chose the one she wanted to go on a date with, the Hessian curtain was pulled back for the lucky winner to face and kiss the lovely Private Dee McCarthy. Unfortunately for the winner, Ritchie replaced Dee at the last minute with an ugly and spotty faced male RAMC Private referred to as 'The Breath Monster'; because he hadn't used a toothbrush since arrival in Iraq he had severe halitosis. According to Ritchie the 'Breath Monsters' arse smelt better than his mouth. The audience roared with laughter and thoroughly enjoyed the whole show; it was a real morale booster for the whole unit.

Corporal Mick Killeen RAMC

It was 0100 hours by the time everyone had traipsed out to the RAF Tristar jet and taken their seats ready for departure. As the aircraft taxied out on to the runway ready for take off the pilot interrupted the chatter in the plane, "Ladies and Gentlemen! There is a remote risk of this aircraft getting hit by Surface to Air missiles whilst in Iraqi airspace." Mick thought 'Why the fuck is he telling me this? If he hadn't mentioned it I would have been in blissful ignorance'. The silence among the passengers was palpable. All the passengers remained silent as the engines roared and the plane started to vibrate as it charged down the runway, the pilot pulled back on the control column and the plane started to lift into the night sky. Everyone on board continued with their impressions of church mice. The plane started to bank as it continued to climb higher and higher and it was still quieter than a Trapist Monk's dining room. After ten minutes the plane levelled out and the pilot informed the passengers, "Ladies and Gentlemen! We are now clear of Iraqi airspace." A massive cheer erupted immediately and the squaddie banter started, "What! You were scared! You fucking wanker, the Iraqis don't have the capability to shoot down an RAF airliner, I wasn't worried at all."

The Tristar landed in Germany six hours later and as Mick looked out of the plane window he was fascinated at how green everything was in Europe, it was overcast weather as they came in to land and dropped off the troops who were returning to Germany. After landing the doors were opened and Mick could smell freshly cut grass, pine trees and dampness, it was a lovely fragrance and Mick today, still thinks of that moment every time he cuts his own grass at home. The UK bound troops continued their journey and disembarked at RAF Brize Norton where it had been raining and puddles of water had formed on the aircraft-parking pan. The lads got off the plane and started dancing in the rain, good old British rain, and they kicked water at each other from the puddles and behaved like over excited children. Mick felt a bit chilly but happy to be back in England.

Captain Sharon Anthony QARANC

As the Regular Army units returned to the UK and BAOR; they just collapsed their tentage, packed up all their equipment and left. The TA soldiers who had served with them throughout the hostilities didn't go with them; the regulars just upped and left them in Iraq and the TA assumed an almost vagrant like status at the airfield and had to fend for themselves. Natalie Baker and three other soldiers who were serving with 3 CS Medical Regiment RAMC came back to their accommodation and found their four cots, sleeping bags and personal kit exactly where they had left it. The massive 18x24 tent that was there before they had gone for lunch; had now been collapsed around their stuff, it had magically disappeared along with all the regular soldiers' cots, sleeping bags, and personal kit that had also been inside the tent next to their own. The whole unit seemed to have disappeared into thin air without so much as a kiss my arse.

Whilst Sharon was at the airfield Headquarters a 4 Tonner pulled up next to her and two young Geordie TA soldiers that she knew, got out of the cab and shouted, "Ma'am…Ma'am… can we have a word with you please!" They had been attached to a Medical Evacuation unit that was going home and had been left in the same predicament as Natalie. After explaining his situation he said, "Where do we go, we don't know what to do now." Sharon reassured them by saying, "Get all your kit and bring it over to our accommodation, you can move in with us until I can sort something out." Sharon reported to RHQ (Regimental Headquarters) to sort this problem out and to find out if she had been allocated a flight back to the UK. Each day she asked the same questions and she always got the same answers, one minute she was told, "Yes you are on a flight today." And the next day it was changed to, "No you are not on a flight today." Before deploying out to Iraq Natalie Baker and her fiancée had made all the arrangements to get married and the wedding date was within the next couple of weeks, if she didn't get a flight back to the UK soon, everything would have to be cancelled at a great financial cost to both of them. Natalie kept going to the Headquarters and nagged, nagged and nagged again about needing to get home for her impending nuptial. Someone obviously got so pissed off with her pleading that she was eventually put on a flight just to get her out of his or her earshot.

Sharon was allocated a seat on a flight about one week after Natalie had flown home in time for her wedding; but she wasn't given much notice when ordered to get herself and all her kit to a certain point at a certain time. At the Headquarters she got access to one of the unit computers and fired off an email to her husband Mick telling him she was coming home, she also got time to go and see Mick Killeen and the other 250 friends she had bumped into at the Field

Hospital. It was an emotionally charged encounter because Mick and the others were not going home; they were staying out in Iraq with the very unit Sharon was leaving. Sharon spent twenty minutes or so saying goodbye to the friends she was recently so happy to see again, she left them, picked up her kit and headed off towards the air conditioned coach that was going to take her to the airport at RAF Kuwait. Sharon was excited about going home to see her family but the feeling of guilt for leaving her friends behind was unbearable.

Lance Corporal Matt Fairclough RAMC

1 CS Medical Regiment RAMC had become non-operational and their Regimental duties were taken over by 3 CS Medical Regiment RAMC. The last of the TA lads from Hull that were attached to 1 CS were now free to go home. Because all their duties and ambulances had been taken over by the 3 CS medics; the soon to be departing medics were just hanging around in the tented accommodation waiting for a flight back to the UK. Matt was summoned over to the Headquarters and warned off for a two day detail to take some vehicles to the docks in Kuwait, he explained to the Headquarters clerk that he was due to fly home with the other TA lads so wouldn't be able to do the detail. The clerk checked the manifest and told Matt, "You're not on the list of soldiers due to fly home, and therefore you are available for the detail. Attend the drivers briefing and you will be detailed a vehicle to drive." Matt went to the briefing and was allocated an M K 4 tonner and trailer to drive without a co-driver, the truck was being shipped back to a unit in Germany, he was also told what kit to bring and what time to parade on the vehicle park. The convoy of vehicles left 1CS at sparrows fart and headed into the desert, the only time they stopped was for comfort breaks so the drivers

could get out of the cab and have a quick piss. Hour after hour Matt just followed the truck in front until as dusk approached; the convoy commander pulled up and everyone laagered up for the night and cooked some rations before getting some much needed sleep. In the morning after doing his ablutions and having a breakfast of tea and several Benson and Hedges fags; Matt tried to start his vehicle but the battery was dead, about fourteen soldiers pushed the MK to bump start it so the wagon could finish the rest of the journey under its own steam.

The convoy arrived at the docks in Kuwait at lunchtime and all the vehicles were lined up nose to tail on a quayside before the drivers had to sanitise every cab and load area. Each vehicle had to be checked for documents and any possible loose ammunition that might be lying around in the trucks. Forty-five minutes later the drivers were herded onto a couple of coaches for the long and uncomfortable journey back to Headquarters 1 CS Medical Regiment; it was impossible to sleep in the cramped seats on the coaches and they all ended up doing impressions of nodding dogs. When they got back to 1 CS Matt was exhausted, he headed straight for his camp bed in the accommodation tent but was stunned to find, all his 5 GS mates had packed up and gone, his was the only camp bed left in the massive 18x24 tent. The last of the 250 Field Ambulance medics he had come to Iraq with had all been put on a flight and flown home. Matt was shocked that he was now the only TA soldier from 250 Field Ambulance still out in Iraq but was too tired to care; he just went to bed.

Sergeant Ritchie John RADC

Ritchie and the other 3 AFA soldiers were told on morning working parade that it was their turn to go home, but first they had to pack up all the units' medical stores and vehicles, and take everything down to the docks at Al Jubayl so it could be shipped back to BAOR in containers. A new sense of urgency seemed to have been miraculously injected into everyone, all the units' medical equipment was packed away in the correct boxes, tents were taken down for the last time and fastidiously packed away in the proper valises, the packing up was supervised by Ritchie, Bob Darkin and all the other Senior NCO's of 3 AFA. On arrival at the docks the unit kit in the wagons was unloaded and stacked near some shipping containers, and the now empty trucks were taken to a another staging area ready to be loaded onto a ship. The loading of the units' boxes and tents was left to an Arabian workforce under the guidance of an Arabian supervisor.

When 3 AFA eventually received the container at their barracks in Sennelager, they discovered the Arabian workforce had opened just about every box and had stolen everything of value. Staff Sergeant Bob Darkin was present when the container was opened in Germany and vented his anger in front of everyone present, "Those thieving fucking bastards, you can't fucking trust any of them." At the bottom of the container they found an unopened box that the Arabs had missed, it contained all of the units' starred items like Binoculars, Compasses and very expensive G1098 watches. When Bob sorted through the equipment he wrote a statement for the RMP's (Royal Military Police) about what he found when the container was opened and he also made a comprehensive list of everything that had been stolen. He then put in a list of deficiencies to the Quartermaster so replacement items could be demanded though the army supply system. The list included Binoculars, Compasses and some very expensive G1098 watches.

Corporal Mick Killeen RAMC

Before leaving Iraq the lads were briefed that they would all have to stay overnight at Chilwell as they were processed through the administrative bullshit of returning to Civvie Street. The medical, pay and other administrative procedures were completed very quickly though and the lads were told transport had already arrived to take them back to Hull. Mick was walking to the camp cookhouse at Chilwell in his combat uniform but wasn't wearing his beret. The RP (Regimental Police) Sergeant nabbed Mick, "Where is your beret? You'll be in deep shit if the RSM sees you, he has a thing about soldiers not wearing headdress." Six months previously Mick would have run off to find his beret to avoid getting into trouble, but on that day he sarcastically said to the RP Sergeant, "Oh right, I'll nip off straight away and dig it out of my Bergen where it has been for the last six months, and I'll plonk it on my head so the RSM doesn't get all upset." Secretly he thought 'I'll chin the twat if he has a go at me'! Mick got into the civilian clothes he had left with the unit prior to deploying out to Iraq. Corporal Gary Dixon RLC was the TA driver of the minibus that had been sent to pick up the lads and return them to Castleford, Hull and Grimsby, Mick recognised him as soon as he walked in the cookhouse and shook his hand.

During the deployment to Iraq some of Mick's comrades had been injured, others were found to be too unfit to continue and there were the usual compassionate cases who had returned early. Of the fifty TA soldiers who left Chilwell to deploy out to Iraq six months previously, only fifteen came back from completing the full tour. The fifteen loaded their kit into the minibus for the final part of the journey home.

Captain Sharon Anthony QARANC

It was a long and boring journey to get from the airfield to RAF Kuwait by coach and when Sharon finally arrived at the combined RAF and US Air Force airport, she was told there was a seven-hour delay in her flight. To pass the time some of the Brits went to the American Forces PX, which is, a version of the British Forces NAAFI (Navy Army Air Force Institute), both have shops and restaurants where service personnel can relax. Sharon and her travelling companions went into the PX to have a look around and were amazed at the sheer size of the place and the variety and quality of provisions on sale. They were thrown out of the building when the Americans realised they were British and not entitled to be in there, but not before they had all stuffed their faces with ice-cream and fruit salad. They then went over to the NAAFI and were very disappointed, but not surprised, by the piss poor standard of the British shopping complex.

When they got on the RAF Tri-Star jet a rotund RAF air steward, wearing overalls, pointed out the emergency exits and demonstrated the seat belts and oxygen masks routine in the event of cabin decompression. Sharon thought he looked a right prat. They landed in Cyprus at 2300 hours and had to get off the plane, they were then penned in a holding area for two hours whilst it was refuelled. Once airborne again the plane headed for Germany to drop off the BAOR based troops and pick up the parents of a casualty who was having treatment in Germany, they then flew to East Midlands airport to drop the parents off at 0600 hours. The plane took off again for the final leg of the journey to RAF Brize Norton, where they landed at 0700 hours. Before Sharon left RAF Kuwait the army told her to change into Desert Camouflage Combat clothing in case the press were there when they all arrived, the MOD (Ministry of Defence) thought it would look better in the papers if all the troops were dressed in the same kit. Sharon refused to do as she was told and stayed in her green combats because the army had really pissed her off by this stage of her tour, they wanted petty things done for their own purposes and yet individuals welfare counted for nothing.

The regular army troops on the plane were welcomed home by their family and friends at RAF Brize Norton, but Sharon and the other eleven TA soldiers on the flight were just given a telephone number by an RAF movements clerk and told to phone up for some transport to come and collect them. It was all a little bit disappointing.

Lance Corporal Matt Fairclough RAMC

Three days after driving a truck to the docks Matt was told by a clerk, "You're on a flight to Gutersloh today, you will be flying back to Germany with one of the BAOR based units." The clerk didn't seem to know or care what would happen to Matt after he had landed in Germany, "You will be their responsibility from that point onwards." The departing soldiers got all their kit on the coaches and headed for Basra International Airport, in the departure lounge Matt was told, "You're not coming with us, you're on a different flight to Brize Norton. See ya!" He joined another group of soldiers who were waiting to go through a departure gate to get on their aircraft, the press were called forward first to board the plane followed by Officers, then SNCO's (Senior Non Commissioned Officers) and lastly the lower ranks were allowed to board. Matt was one of the last to board the RAF VC 10 aircraft and as he walked towards the plane a soldier from the Queens Lancashire Regiment followed him. The infantryman's' skin was a whiter shade of white and everyone else getting on the plane had skin the colour of tanned hide, the QLR explained that he had only arrived in Iraq about a week earlier and was the first soldier from his battalion to go home on R and R (Rest and Recuperation).

When Matt buckled up his seat belt he felt someone tap him on the shoulder, it was one of the VC 10's air stewards, "Hiya Matt! How the hell are you, I haven't seen you since we went on the piss at RAF Honnington." Matt immediately recognised his old friend George; they had served together at RAF Honnington before Matt had left the RAF. There wasn't much time to catch up on the old days and even though Matt was a low priority on the passenger list, George and the other air stewards gave him the VIP treatment when it came to drinks and meals.

Sergeant Ritchie John RADC

After the units' equipment and vehicles had been left at the docks in Al Jubayl, 3 AFA were transported in coaches to some comfortable transit barracks, the large, clean, and airy dormitory rooms had rows of bunk beds, and each bed had a mattress and pillow. The toilets and shower rooms were again, all very clean and spacious, the medics and 'Gob Doctors' basked in the luxury of hot showers, flushing toilets, and a comfy bed to sleep on. There were no duties for the lads to do so they were bussed into Kuwait City to have a good look around, buy souvenirs, and get themselves a decent meal in a Kuwaiti restaurant. Ritchie also took the opportunity to phone his mum and dad and let them know he would be coming home soon, they were pleased to hear from him and relieved that he was coming home unscathed.

As he and Bob Darkin walked past a hotel in the city centre a local Kuwaiti man stopped them; he shook their hands and

218

thanked them for liberating his country from the Iraqi army. In his gratitude he offered to buy them both a meal, it was the very least he could do for them; they had shown such great courage and bravely fought to free his country from the invading Iraqi Army. He would not be put off by their protestations and herded the two of them into a Burger King style fast food outlet, and he sat there whilst they both ate a Hamburger, French Fries and a bucket of cola. Ritchie felt a bit of a fraud for accepting this heartfelt generosity; he didn't feel he had done anything to deserve such praise.

A couple of days later Ritchie queued up with the other lads from 3 AFA to board a British Airways 747 in Kuwait airport, dust bins were provided by the British Military authorities for soldiers to dump any firearms, knives and ammunition that they might be trying to smuggle back to Germany. They were all told that the penalties for not surrendering weapons of any type during this amnesty would be severe. Lance Corporal Steve Mercer RADC was standing next to Ritchie as they went through the farce of giving their name and showing their Identity Cards to a Movements Clerk, so they could be ticked off on a list before getting on board the plane. The departure lounge in the early hours of the morning was reasonably cool and yet Steve Mercer was sweating and looked anxious and slightly uncomfortable, Ritchie was concerned that Steve was about to do something stupid like smuggle a weapon onboard the aircraft. He needn't have worried though because Steve had no interest in weaponry at all, however, using his underpants as a hiding place, he was stupid enough to try smuggling the lizards from his farm onto the aircraft.

On the seven and a half hour flight to Hanover, beer was served with the in-flight meals and because the medics hadn't had any alcohol since leaving Germany four months earlier, they became drunk quite quickly. This resulted in the BA airhostesses being groped and goosed every time they walked up and down the aisle serving drinks and meals, they were very professional and good natured though and just smiled through all the molestations and double entendre. By the time they landed at Hanover Airport at 0900 hours the medics were pissed as old farts and staggered down the aircraft mobile steps wearing the airhostesses' scarves, hats, and jackets. The General Officer Commanding was at Hanover Airport to welcome his units' back to BAOR, he was not amused.

Corporal Mick Killeen RAMC

Corporal Garry Dixon pulled up inside the gates of Wenlock Barracks in Hull, the Castleford lot had already been dropped off and now it was the lads from Hulls' turn. Families and friends were there to meet them but Jean wasn't, Mick had only phoned her half an hour earlier to let her know he wasn't staying over night at Chilwell as planned and could she pick him up in the car. None of the returning soldiers hung around, they quickly got into their cars and bomb burst into different directions and headed home. The minibus drove out of the camp gates to take the last of the returning soldier's home to Grimsby and Mick was left alone with his kit under the gathering rain clouds. It was early evening and Mick shivered because of the cold and damp weather, he placed his Bergen on a bit of the car park that wasn't covered in puddles and sat down to wait for Jean to arrive. Mick was staring up at the RCT classroom where he had started his TA career all those years ago when Richie, the unit MT Staff Sergeant came round the corner. Richie had detailed the minibus to pick up the returning soldiers and had waited in his office for them to arrive. Mick thought 'What a nice fella, he could have been at home with his feet up but, no, he had stayed of his own volition to see us back'. Jock Carragher the unit cook came through the camp gates and also came up to chat to Mick, a couple of minutes later Jean drove in through the camp entrance with Rachael and pulled up next to Mick. Mick said, "Sorry lads but my family are here and I haven't seen them for six months." They both said goodbye and disappeared as quickly as possible.

Rachel ran towards her dad and cried buckets as she hugged him, Jean was equally emotional and the three of them held on to each other as if their very life depended on it. They then got into the car and Mick went home.

Captain Sharon Anthony QARANC

Sharon's husband Mick went into Wenlock Barracks to find out what arrangements had been made to collect the returning TA soldiers from Chilwell once they had been through the demob processing. The NRPS (Non Regular Permanent Staff) Admin Officer, Captain Frost (who was an ex- regular army officer), told Mick that Sharon wasn't coming back yet, he ordained, "The Ministry of Defence would have informed me in the first instance." Mick started to get angry and reiterated "Sharon and at least one other TA soldier from 250 are back in the UK; as we speak they are on their way to Chilwell and will be ready to be picked up in the next few hours." Even after telling Frost that he had spoken to Sharon on her mobile phone as she stood in the arrival lounge at Brize Norton, Frost would not be budged; he would do nothing until the MOD had confirmed that Sharon had officially arrived back in the UK. Mick took matters into his own hands, he drove out of Wenlock Barracks and headed to the nearest petrol station, he then filled up with fuel and set off for Chilwell without waiting to hear from the Ministry of Defence.

Sharon and the other TA lads arrived for their demob processing on a minibus that the staff at Chilwell had sent to collect them from Brize Norton. It was about 1100 hours by the time Sharon got through most of her demob administration, she filled out a survey which asked questions like, "Did you see anything bad? Do you think you are suffering from PTSD (Post Traumatic Stress Disorder)?" Sharon says, "Even if you ticked yes in any of the boxes they didn't do anything about it apart from telling you not to get drunk, she was warned that if she did get drunk the chances were, she might start shouting and hitting people, but not to worry, this is quite natural after going to war."

On completing the demob farce Sharon walked over to the car park to see if Mick had arrived, she saw him walking towards her but as they approached each other he blanked her and walked straight past. He didn't recognise his own wife because she was heavily tanned, had sun-bleached blonde hair and had lost two stone in weight; she also looked gaunt and very tired. Says Sharon, "It wasn't a very romantic re-union, Mick didn't pick me up and spin me round like they do in the movies, we just kissed and hugged each other and Mick asked where the rest of my kit was." The other TA soldier who had travelled with Sharon was an ex regular army Lance Corporal called Craig, and as Captain Frost wasn't going to send any transport to collect him either, Mick said he would give Craig a lift back home to Castleford. Mick drove into Castleford town centre and asked Craig for directions to the house where Craig and his wife lived, he replied, "Oh, just drop me here at my social club, I'm going to have a couple of pints before I go and see our lass."

Mick then took Sharon home.

Lance Corporal Matt Fairclough RAMC

Matt landed at RAF Brize Norton and after going through the customs area he was put on a minibus with several other TA soldiers from units around the UK, they were then transported up to Chilwell to be demobbed from their attachment to the Regular British Army. At a motorway service station Matt phoned his dad Harry to let him know he was now back in England, and could he do him a favour and phone Wenlock Barracks to arrange some transport to pick him up from Chilwell. When Harry phoned 250 Field Ambulance he was told there wasn't anyone in authority available to make the command decision of dispatching a Land Rover to pick up Matt from Chilwell, so Harry set off to do it himself.

By the time Harry arrived at the demob centre Matt had just about finished his final documentation process, they bumped into each other in the unit car park. Matt had always been a skinny kid when he was younger and had maintained a racing snake build throughout his military careers in the RAF and Territorial Army. But on that day Harry thought Matt's body looked emaciated, his green combat clothing was literally just hanging onto his physical structure; he looked tanned but very tired. After hugging each other Matt and Harry went to get his kit and loaded it into the car before setting off for Beverley, the pair of them had to stop in another service station because Harry was diabetic and needed to get something to eat. Seven miles outside of Beverley in a small village called South Cave; Matt asked Harry to pull over into the car park of the White Hart pub, he hadn't had a beer in the last six months and wanted one now. As the pub landlady pulled a pint of Stella Artois for Matt and a Diet Coke for Harry she asked Matt, "Have you just got back from Iraq?" Matt replied, "Yep!" She handed over the pint of lager to Matt and said, "Well, this one is on the house." After thanking his host Matt licked his lips and sank the pint of cold beer in one long drawn out and enjoyable sequence of gulps, he then placed the empty glass on the bar and belched longer and louder than anything Homer Simpson had ever managed to achieve. The men in the pub applauded.

Harry then bought Matt a second Pint of Stella which he drank at a much more leisurely pace, before leaving the pub they again thanked the landlady for her hospitality and Harry drove home with the last soldier from Hull (250) B Squadron 5 GS Medical Regiment RAMC to get back from Iraq.

Sergeant Ritchie John RADC

A line of German civilian contracted coaches were parked in Hanover Airport car park, the majority of them were going straight to 3 AFA's barracks in Sennelager, the odds and sods attached to 3 AFA to make the unit up their wartime establishment were allocated a single coach to return them all to their respective Garrisons around BAOR. Ritchie went round as many of the unit as he could to say his goodbyes, he made a point of searching out Bob Darkin as he wanted to shake hands with him before he got on his coach, Ritchie would be leaving the army soon and it might be the last time they saw each other. The usual squaddie banter kicked in as Bob called Ritchie a moaning wanker, to which Ritchie said he was going to be glad to see the back of not just Bob, but the whole of 3 fucking AFA. The Sennelager bound coaches set off down the autobahn with the 3 AFA medics on board, at the same time their families and friends were gathering just inside the barrack gates in Sennelager to

224

welcome them home. It took a couple of hours to travel from Hanover to Sennelager and even though everyone on the coaches was exhausted from their journey, they were all eager to see their wives, sons and daughters. At about 1500 hours the OC spoke to the driver of the coach as they drove in towards the Sennelager Training area and asked him to pull up and park outside the camp gates, he then spoke to the SQMS, Staff Sergeant Mick Germaine, and told him he wanted everyone to debus and parade in three ranks, the unit would then march into camp in front of all their families and friends with the OC at the head of the parade. Mick was incensed by the idea and told the OC as such, "You want us all to do a victory march into the camp like conquering fucking heroes, when in reality, all we've done for four months is sit in the desert on our fat fucking arses getting a sun tan! Sir, you can do what you want, I'm going to see my family." And without further ado Mick disembarked the coach and walked off to go and meet his family. The OC had his parade without the presence of Staff Sergeant Mick Germaine.

At about the same time Ritchie was arriving in Osnabruck Garrison and after leaving the coach he headed off to see if anyone was working in the Dental Centre. He had a cup of tea and a chat with some of the staff before making his way to the Sergeant's Mess and was allocated a transit room to bed down in until a more permanent room could be arranged for him at a later date. After making his bed Ritchie lay down on it and said, "Ah! Lovely." He slept for a couple of hours and then went down town and got pissed on three pints of German Lager; he caught a taxi back to camp and went to bed. In the morning Ritchie went on leave and flew to Belfast to visit his mum and dad.

Epilogues

Mr Mick Killeen

When Mick opened his call up papers ordering him to deploy out to Iraq, there was a mixture of emotions and opinions within the immediate Killeen family. Jean had been a TA soldiers wife for a long time and was accustomed to Mick going away for a couple of weeks annually for his TA Summer Camp, but unwittingly for Jean, this six month separation would be the longest time they had ever spent apart. Moaning about what they were going to endure was not an option for both Mick and Jean, he had signed up to serve in the British Army, and they both felt quite strongly that he must do his duty. They felt this way even though Mick was going to be sent thousands of miles away and there was a very real possibility that he could get killed, and not necessarily by enemy action. Soldiers often get killed on Military Exercises in accidents due to night moves, increased traffic flow, and lack of concentration because of extreme tiredness. When the British Army deploys for war, these hazards are magnified tenfold. Whilst Mick was away, Jean would have to take sole responsibility for every domestic, financial, and emotional problem that she, Rachael and Victoria may have to face. Jean was also aware that it would be unfair of her to write to Mick about any trivial problems she may have, particularly whilst he was serving in a war zone. He would more than likely be extremely tired, busy, and at times, very scared, with all this on his plate Jean didn't want Mick worrying about what was happening at home. There probably wasn't a lot he could do to help anyway. Jean also had to appear nonchalant about their situation for the sake of the two girls; if Jean didn't show any concern then hopefully the girls would feel the same way. Jean kept up this charade until Mick came home, even though at times she was very scared herself.

Rachael was there when Mick opened the call up envelope but didn't believe for one moment that he would actually go out to Iraq and play a part in the war. She didn't agree with the war at the time and still doesn't today, but she is adamant that everyone should support the troops that have to go out and do the Governments' dirty work. "If the British Government says we went out there to free the Iraqi people from Saddam Hussein, then why aren't we out in Zimbabwe getting rid of Robert Mugabe? We all know the answer, Zimbabwe doesn't produce any oil!"

The same evening Mick read his orders 18 year old Victoria was going out on her first date with new boyfriend Jamie, so Mick, Jean, and Rachael decided not to tell her about it until the following morning. They knew she would be upset and it would probably have ruined her evening. She cried when they told her and was very upset at the thought of Mick not being there for the foreseeable future, and anyway she thought, 'My Dad is far too old to go and fight in a war'. The MOD didn't think so. Victoria remarks, "The United States Navy, Army and Air Force is massive, so why did they need us out there, I don't think he should have gone."

Mick wrote home as soon after deploying as he possibly could and several weeks later mentioned in one letter that he hadn't received any letters from home. Rachael was upset at this news as she had sent loads of bluey's (a fold up MOD Form type letter that can be sealed) but they were obviously not getting through to where Mick was stationed. A friend of hers mentioned that it was possible to send out email bluey's to Mick on a link through the British Forces Website, Mick could open these emails at Headquarters 5 GS in Iraq about 5 hours after they had been sent.

Mail has always been important to soldiers serving away from their families and once the British Forces Postal System had eventually been set up, the mail arrived regularly. Jean and the girls sent out parcels trying to fulfil Mick's wish lists as best they could, muesli bars, baby wipes, toothpaste and brushes, tinned fruit, dried fruit and any sort of sweets that wouldn't melt in the heat of the desert was gratefully received. Jean was concerned that Mick would get into trouble for the bottle of brandy he requested as alcohol was taboo in the state of Iraq. Mick reassured her in his next letter by saying, "The worst thing they can do to me is send me home, so put some brandy in the post!" The medium sized bottle of brandy was shared with the other Crew Members when they made a brew.

At home Mick has had to get used to being surrounded by women, living with a wife and two daughters should have entitled him to some sort of gallantry award even before going out to Iraq. But his Female Restricted Sanctuary whilst in residence is at the foot of his large and very neat garden, Mick has turned his garage into a workshop and the 'bolted from the inside' side door that opens up into the garden has a spy hole fitted in it. If any femmes fatales dare knock on that door says Mick, "She had better come bearing a large mug of tea." Rachael spotted a book in WH Smiths called 'Men and their Sheds' which she sent out to Iraq for Mick. When he opened the book some of the daffodils from his garden fell out, Jean had pressed them in between the pages.

All the families of the Hull soldiers serving out in Iraq were given briefings in Wenlock Barracks by the units Regular Army Training Officer; he displayed a large map of Iraq on the wall and explained where the men were and what they were doing. It was also a chance for the wives to ask any questions and air any problems they were having that the unit may be able to help them with. Money was a major concern for Jean as Mick was not at work with British Aerospace and she was unsure when the MOD would start putting Mick's army pay into the bank. "British Aerospace were absolutely brilliant" says Jean, "They continued paying his wages for a while after he had gone and also paid all his Share and Health Schemes whilst he was away, to top it all off British Aerospace allowed Mick his full entitlement of holidays when he came back to work."

The Yorkshire Bank assured Jean that all their Standing Orders would be paid even if the wages were late coming in; the first MOD payment amounted to £16, and the second £28. Three days later £2,000 was paid into the account and from then on payments were received monthly without fail.

Jean and the two girls missed Mick dreadfully during his tour away during which he missed Rachael's 21st birthday, Victoria's 'A' level results and his Nieces' wedding when she came over from America. Jean had to be mother and father whilst Mick was away and says, "With two young daughters I had to be both parents, and you can't let your emotions, fear and worries get in the way, you have to put them to one side and get on with everything." When asked if it was hard for her when Mick was away Jean got very emotional, "Every single bloody day was hard, if the girls saw me get upset they would have been the same, so I had to be strong. Mick and I only had two weeks to get ready for him going to war, and yes, it was hard, every second of it."

When Jean and Rachael drove towards Wenlock Barracks to pick Mick up, Jean started thinking about 'what are we going to talk about, what shall I say to him when I first see him'. Rachael was out of the car door and running towards her dad before Jean had even stopped the car. They were both shocked when they saw how much weight Mick had lost and how drawn his face was, before he left he was stick thin but with the added weight loss he looked terminally ill. Victoria was on holiday in Spain and phoned Jean occasionally to make sure she was OK, when Mick answered the phone she was astonished and asked, "What are you doing there?" When she ultimately arrived home from her holiday she copied Rachael's stuntman actions and tried to leap from the minibus before it came to a halt. Victoria's girlfriends who accompanied her on the holiday and were also travelling in the minibus cried as she threw herself into her dad's arms.

Mick spent a lot of time in the garden when he got back, he seemed to be fascinated by how green everything was, he also had a bit of trouble adjusting to not having a personal weapon at his side every moment of the day and night. Jean woke up early one morning to find Mick fumbling around under the bed, "I wouldn't have minded if he was fumbling with me but he seemed to be looking for something." A tired and confused Mick kept asking, "Where is my rifle?" Other than these minor behavioural curiosities Mick settled back into home life almost immediately, Jean had no problem talking to Mick at all; in fact it felt like he had never been away.

The first Remembrance Sunday after returning from Iraq was made an obligatory training weekend by the OC of Hull (250) B Squadron 5 GS Medical Regiment, and it was also made a Friday night start which infuriated Jean. The Commanding Officer of Wenlock Barracks could ponce about for the Weekend at a Remembrance Parade, but when his men had returned from the war in Iraq he couldn't be bothered to come to Wenlock Barracks and welcome them home. This insult left Mick feeling humiliated and angry for all of the lads from Hull; they had gone to war and carried the name of 250 Field Ambulance with pride. They had done a good job and no one could have asked for more. In the Regular British Army most men retire from soldiering at the age of 40, Mick was 50 years old. After soldiering for real in the Gulf War, Mick felt it would be futile to play at soldiers on Drill Nights and weekend Exercises, he had read the book, seen the film and now genuinely, acted in the play. It was time to leave.

Eighteen months after returning home Mick received another letter from the MOD asking him to confirm his home address so they could forward his Gulf War Medal to him. Mick didn't reply to the letter, as he believes medals should be given for acts of Gallantry not for just turning up and taking part. Jean and the girls felt differently, they are immensely proud of Mick and wish that he had accepted the medal, Jean thinks it would be nice to pass on to any future grandchildren and she was tempted to forge Mick's signature (apparently she's been doing it for years) on the form but it was Mick's decision and they would all abide by it.

During the final interview for this book Mick was asked if he thought the Second Gulf War was worth it, he replied, "I don't have an opinion, I'm not allowed one. I was a soldier who had signed on the dotted line and I had to go regardless of whether I thought it was right or wrong. Having said that, I don't think it was about freeing the Iraqi people, of that I am sure. It was all about the Ramallah Oil Fields that 1 Para captured straight away, one fifth of the worlds oil supply is there and the US wanted to have control of it. There were no WMD and the Iraqi Armed Forces didn't have the means of delivery to hit the UK anyway, they could just about hit

Israel." When asked if they would go through the whole thing again if required, unsurprisingly, they both emphatically replied, "Yes!"

Mick continues to work for British Aerospace.

Mrs Sharon Anthony

Before Sharon deployed out to Iraq her husband Mick told her, "Trust no-one! Our side, their side, any bloody side, they will all shit on you, you've got to start getting hard and look after yourself or you're going to get hurt!" It was probably good advice from a tough rugby playing ex TA soldier with about fifteen year's experience of peacetime soldiering. Mick explains, "Lets face it, Sharon wasn't really squaddie material, she trusted everyone and took what they said at face value, she couldn't see the negative side of people and was incredibly naive." He goes on, "There's nothing wrong with that, its part of her personality, but in a violent situation you need to be aware of who is the most likely person to hurt you and Sharon didn't have that in her psyche."

In the early stages though, Sharon thought Mick's advice was superfluous because the general consensus before she went down to Beckingham Training Camp, was that the TA would take over and man all the UK military medical establishments and let the Regular Army Medics go off to war. At a push she might get a chance to go off to a camp in Germany or Cyprus and make a bit of a holiday out of her deployment. Sharon's children, Donna, who was twenty one years old and in her 2nd year studies at university, and Stephen, who is a Civil Engineer, came home to see their mum because she would be leaving within the next week and it was still unclear exactly where she was going to deploy. The four of them went round to see Sharon's parents so she could say goodbye to them, her dad Harry got upset at the thought of his daughter going off to war. He was probably thinking about what he went through in the Korean War and was obviously aware of the subsequent ordeals she might have to experience.

Just before Sharon actually flew out of South Cerney airport and headed for Iraq, she had to plug her mobile telephone into a cigarette machine plug socket in the airport reception area, her phone was low on power, and she wanted to speak to Mick before she got on the flight. That very day was their wedding anniversary and she was flying into the unknown, she would be leaving her beloved husband and children behind and didn't know if she would ever see them again. Sharon got Mick on the phone and bade him goodbye but she didn't have the emotional strength to phone Stephen and Donna to do the same. Sharon says, "It was too hard." Whilst discussing this during the final interview with Sharon and her family, Sharon got very emotional; she turned to her daughter and said, "I'm sorry Donna." Seven years later and it is still hard for Sharon to talk about the emotionally charged moment when she had to leave her family and face what fate was going to throw at her. "I would like to publicly say sorry to both Donna and Stephen for not saying goodbye properly, I don't even want to think about how they would have felt had the unthinkable happened and I had not spoken to them before flying out to Iraq. They would have been devastated." As parents, Sharon and Mick obviously wanted to protect their children from any worry and hurt, but in doing this; it left Donna feeling isolated and slightly alienated. Like her mother, Donna is an intelligent young woman and was aware of what was going on, in reality, the '1 Close Support Regiment RAMC' address where she sent all her letters to Sharon really gave it away. And anyway, wherever Sharon deployed in Iraq would involve her being exposed to some level of danger regardless of where she was serving in the ORBAT (Order of Battle).

Donna knew her brother was getting as much information as he could from their dad, so when the siblings talked on the phone, Donna made sure Stephen told her everything he knew. She drove her boyfriend to distraction because she watched Sky Television News every day in the hope of catching a snippet of information about the Scots Dragoon Guards, to whom she knew Sharon was attached. Donna also shared university digs in a house with one of David Blunketts' sons (During the Second Gulf War David Blunkett was Home Secretary) and she hounded him to speak to his father about where Sharon was and to make sure she was all right. These persistent demands obviously came to nothing. The night before Sharon left for Beckingham Training Area Donna and Stephen had surreptitiously placed mother's day cards in Sharon's Bergen because they knew their mother wouldn't be at home on the day itself. Sharon found the cards before she even left the UK but didn't open them; she knew what they were and sentimentally wanted to save them so she could open them on Mothers Day proper. Sharon says, "Mothers Day was horrible, I was out in Iraq and not only was I away from my family but I didn't even have any friends in the unit that I could talk too. When I opened the cards from Donna and Stephen they contained photographs of my mum and dad, Mick, Stephen and Donna. It was absolutely heartbreaking." The Padre, Captain Ian Richardson, was on hand though and he told Sharon, "Get in the back of that 4 tonner and let it all go, have a really good cry and don't worry, I'll keep everyone away from you until you feel better." And that's exactly what Sharon did. Donna is immensely proud of what her mother has done and is the first to admit, there is no way she could have gone through the same experiences, "I like to have nail varnish, hair straighteners and a bathroom within easy reach. Her dad Mick confirmed this when he said, "I was surprised Donna survived the Glastonbury festival!"

Unlike his sister, Stephen didn't write to his mum every day, he saved his letters up and wrote only occasionally but at great length. Mick did write every day but Sharon didn't want to hear about all the information coming from Sky TV; she's a woman and just wanted the day to day gossip of what was going on back in Hull, so Mick had to step out of his normal macho role and tell Sharon about all the local scandal in their neighbourhood. At one stage he ran out of things to write about and told Sharon that next doors cat had started shitting in their garden. He was also getting some strange looks from the checkout girls at the local supermarket because he turned up several times a week to buy women's panties (albeit the wrong sizes), it was lucky for Sharon that Donna was sending her the correct size underwear. He also sent T shirts, sports bras and all the gossipy magazines he could lay his hands on, he also sent Sharon an England rugby shirt to wear during the units' PT sessions. Sharon states quite categorically, "We were attached to a Scottish Armoured Regiment, there was no way on this earth that I would have been brave enough to wear that shirt in front of them."

On her return to the UK Sharon told Mick she didn't want a great deal of fuss made when she got home, she just wanted to be with her close family. Mick complied with her wishes but to this day he still regrets not putting some bunting up on the outside of their house and getting their neighbours to welcome her home. He and Sharon feel that members of 250 Field Ambulance in Hull have been shabbily treated by the MOD and their own unit, the lack of transport to pick them up for one thing and the fact that not one of the upper echelon in Wenlock Barracks could be bothered to greet them when they came back to Hull. They had flown the flag of their TA unit whilst serving alongside the ranks of the Regular British Army and had done the job they were sent to do with professionalism and pride. The Commanding Officer of Hull (250) B Squadron 5 GS Medical Regiment was lucky enough not to have to deploy out to Iraq so you would think he could have spared just an hour or so to welcome his troops back home, this is why Mick wishes he had organised his own welcome home parade for Sharon.

The TA seemed surreal to Sharon after her experiences on a real operational tour and she made herself absent from more and more Drill Nights, in fact she never went on another TA Field Exercise.

Eighteen months after she got back from Iraq Sharon got a phone call from a TA Sergeant at 250 Field Ambulance asking if she had received her Gulf War Medal, when she told him she hadn't he gave her the telephone number of the 'medal place in Gloucester', he told her, "You should give them a ring and find out why they haven't sent yours out, I've already got mine." Sharon rang the telephone number and gave the clerk at the other end of the line her number, rank, and name and asked when she would receive her medal. The clerk told Sharon, "We sent your medal to Wenlock Barracks about eight months ago." On phoning Wenlock Barracks Sharon was told both hers and Natalie's' medals had been in the unit safe since the unit had received them, "If you want them, give the new NRPS (Non Regular Permanent Staff) officer a ring and arrange a time and date to come and collect them." A date and time was arranged with the new unit officer and he told Sharon she could pick up Natalie's medal at the same time. When Sharon turned up at Wenlock Barracks on the designated day she was told by one of the admin clerks, "Oh sorry, the NRPS officer has gone out for a run and won't be back for a while, I'll get the medals for you." The clerk pulled open the draw to her desk, grabbed the medals, and threw them on the desk, "Sign for them on this piece of paper will you." And that was how Sharon and Natalie were presented with their Gulf War Medals, no parade, no handshake, not even a pat on the back. The soldiers that came back after the Falklands War and the soldiers returning from Afghanistan today are hailed as hero's, in 1982 and today these returning warriors parade through the local town and receive plaudits from around the country. Sharon doesn't deny them these deserved honours but she feels that the TA sneaked back into the UK without any public recognition of what they had achieved.

Sharon wrote and protested to John Prescott the Hull MP about the lack of equipment, the need for proper training of soldiers before they deploy on operational tours and also about the lack of recognition for all TA soldiers who had served in Iraq. She got a reply from some menial in his constituency office who stated, "John Prescott MP does not deal with North Hull, he is an East Hull MP, you should write to Mr Kevin McNamara MP." Sharon thought, 'Bugger it, this is pointless, no-one is going to listen and they will probably care even less'. At the time of writing this book the Iraq War enquiry is ongoing but Sharon firmly believes nothing will be proven and Tony Blair and all the other politicians will carry on with their sanctimonious lives oblivious of how their decisions affect real people. The millions of pounds spent on this farcical showcase will prove, in the words of Sharon, "Nothing at all. My life and my family's lives were put on hold, and for what? We as soldiers knew we shouldn't have been out there, we knew it was wrong but the Iraq War protestors vented their anger on the troops who have to carry out the Government of the days policies. It wasn't our fault and they shouldn't have had a go at us. Those protestors were being disrespectful to the wrong people!"

Asked if she would go again if the need arose, Sharon states, "Yes I probably would, but I would go out there with a totally different attitude, the blood and gore didn't bother me as much as it did other people I worked with, but how human beings can be so cruel and violent to each other is very difficult to mentally absorb."

Sharon has had a few emotional problems after getting back from Iraq and because of her experiences out there, she now puts up an imaginary brick wall all around her if she comes under any pressure. She continues to work with an NHS drug rehabilitation programme.

Mr Matt Fairclough

For the first three nights after coming back from Iraq, Matt stayed with Harry and his girlfriend Nicky at their house in Beverley; he spent the majority of that time watching television; it was something that seemed to mesmerise him. On the fourth day Matt told Harry that he wanted to go and visit Leanne; a female pen friend who had started writing to him whilst he was out in Iraq, Leanne and her five-year-old daughter Sasha lived on the other side of the country in Oldham. Harry wasn't concerned as he dropped Matt off at Beverley railway station; Matt seemed to be quite happy and was looking forward to meeting Leanne for the first time. It was three weeks before Matt got in touch with Harry and informed him he had moved in with Leanne and her daughter; he also told Harry that Oldham was, "A fucking shit hole, but at least it was only a pound a pint in most of the working men's clubs." Within the next few months Matt also joined the local Royal Engineer TA unit as their Squadron medic, the Training Officer was quite keen to recruit him into their unit and he dealt with all the formalities of his transfer to them from 250 Field Ambulance, Matt retained his Lance Corporal rank. He did medical cover on Squadron Exercises and Range Days, and also gave first aid training to the Sappers in the unit.

Within six months things started to go wrong for Matt, he found he couldn't sleep at night and became nervous and depressed for no apparent reason, his SSM (Squadron Sergeant Major) had noticed that Matt seemed irritable on most Drill Nights and called him into his office for a chat. "Is everything ok Matt? You seem a bit out of sorts lately?" Matt assured him he was all right but the SSM wasn't convinced and told Matt that he would help him in any way he could. The tenderness of this reputedly tough soldier seemed to get to Matt and he started to cry, Matt left the office after telling the SSM that he was ok, but if he needed any help he would definitely confide in him. He didn't though.

On the 1st of July, nearly a year after returning from Iraq, Leanne threw a party for Matt in their house and invited about fifteen people to celebrate his thirty fourth birthday, Matt used his skills as a chef and put together a buffet for the party and laid on the music which was very loud. By midnight Matt had only had a few drinks, he was feeling tired and told Leanne that he was going to bed and left everyone else downstairs to carry on with the party. Leanne went up stairs fifteen minutes later to check on him and found Matt trying to commit suicide using a dressing gown cord, although horrified by this spectacle she ran downstairs for a knife and cut the cord, she also told everyone to leave as the party was now over. Matt came round and started shouting obscenities at no one in particular and he smashed up the wardrobe doors before walking out of the house, Leanne chased after him and eventually persuaded Matt to come back to the house. In the meantime Leanne's father who lived a couple of doors away had phoned the police and asked for help, a male constable arrived with a female colleague and asked Leanne "What exactly is the problem?" She told him, "It's my boyfriend, he's had some problems lately, and I think it's all to do with his time in the Iraq War." After making sure no one had been injured they went into the lounge and found Matt sitting on the sofa and visibly shaking, the Policeman asked him "Would you like some help?" Matt nodded his head and was led out to the police car, as he was helped into the back of the vehicle he asked the policewoman, "I'm not being arrested am I?" She re-assured him that he wasn't and they were just going to get him some help.

At the A&E Department in Oldham hospital the police officers stayed with Matt and told him not to apologise, they were there to give assistance to anyone who needed it, and they felt that Matt definitely needed help. A Duty Psychiatrist did some observational tests on Matt and left him on his own in a side room until 0700 hours when he told Matt that he should be admitted to hospital for further evaluation. Unfortunately there weren't any spare beds at Oldham Hospital so the nursing staff at the A&E Department transferred Matt to a Psychiatric Ward in a Stockport Hospital and diagnosed as suffering from acute PTSD (Post Traumatic Stress Disorder). As he was being transported to Stockport in an ambulance, the irony of the situation was not totally lost on Matt as he remembered the US Marine psychiatric patient he escorted to a Field Hospital when he was out in Iraq. It was three days before a spare bed could be found for Matt at Oldham hospital. Leanne phoned Harry who came over to see her and he went to the hospital to visit Matt, Leanne's father told Harry that Matt could not hold a conversation with anyone unless he was talking about the Iraq War, "At first it was quite interesting but after all this time he is just boring everyone to death. He's got to get over it and get on with his life."

Matt was in and out of hospital for the next few months and was given several types of medication to calm his nerves and stop the depression. After four months Leanne had had enough, it wasn't good for her daughter to live in this fragile sort of environment and she quite rightly asked Matt to leave. Although Harry had been over to Oldham several times to visit Matt at home and in hospital, the situation was untenable for Matt, he was embarrassed about his condition and so contacted his mother Ronnie, to ask if he could stay with her and her husband in Bridlington, he was ashamed of himself and didn't want Harry to see him again until he had sorted his problems out. Matt was discharged from Oldham hospital the day before Christmas Eve 2004 and went to visit his sister who was living in Blyth near Newcastle; Ronnie arranged the rail ticket for Matt to get to Newcastle where he spent Christmas with Ronnie, Naomi, Daniel and all their associated family members. After Christmas Matt travelled with Ronnie and her husband to Bridlington and stayed with them for about a year, one of the conditions for his release from hospital was that Matt had to contact the local psychiatric services at Bridlington hospital to continue with his treatment. He was assigned a Community Psychiatric Nurse called Bob Tidy to help him; Bob would pick Matt up from the house and take him out for coffee and a chat. Bob encouraged Matt to talk about anything from, the war in Iraq, to how he was getting his laundry done. The subject was irrelevant; Matt needed to communicate with people on a variety of matters.

Ronnie had worked as a ward assistant in the Psychiatric Ward in Bridlington Hospital for a short while, and although she only dished out meals and made beds, she felt she was qualified enough to know what was best for Matt. A little knowledge is a very dangerous thing, and to make matters worse Ronnie was telling just about anyone who would listen about what Matt was going through. Matt discussed his concerns about his mum blabbing to other people with Bob, he also told him he was going back up to Newcastle to visit his sister Naomi for a couple of weeks to get away from her. Whilst he was away Bob made a discreet visit to Ronnie's house on the pretext of visiting Matt and he spent about half an hour there talking to Ronnie. When Matt returned from Newcastle and met up with Bob on his next scheduled appointment, Bob said, "We have got to get you out of that house, you cannot stay there any longer. There is a Mind (Mind is a mental heath charity in England and Wales) Hostel in Bridlington where patients can stay in self-contained flats and help each other dealing with day-to-day issues, I'm going to try and get you a placement in there." All patients are allowed to stay in the hostel for a minimum of six months and up to a maximum of two years; they have to pay a small amount of rent and are held responsible for keeping their rooms clean and tidy and paying all their own bills. Psychiatric Health Staff are on call to help everyone in the hostel twenty-four hours a day.

Matt's mental health and confidence improved with the help of Bob and the hostel staff and eventually, Matt ended up giving cooking lessons to the other residents in the hostel, he planned his lessons and asked those taking part what they wanted to cook. It was of benefit to all concerned. The hostel was a no go area for Matt's mum and in fact the first visitors he invited to the flat was Harry and his girlfriend Nicky, both of whom were amazed at his psychological improvement.

On one of his visits up to Newcastle Matt met Naomi's neighbour Donna and her son. They started a relationship but it was fragmented because Matt had to return to the hostel after each visit. Donna asked him to move up to Blyth and live with her and her son but Matt was reluctant after what had occurred with Leanne over in Oldham. It took Donna over a year to convince Matt to move in with her; in November 2006 Harry hired a Transit van and helped Matt move all his possessions from the hostel up to Blyth.

Matt, Donna and her son are still living together and Matt has started working a couple of days a week at the St George Psychiatric Hospital in Morpeth as a Support Volunteer, he talks to patients about their problems and how he personally has learned to cope with things.

Superintendent Ritchie John

For the first two weeks of his post Iraq war leave Ritchie stayed at his parent's home in Carnlough, a small coastal village north of Belfast; he spent most of that time working with his dad at his Market Gardening Business. He then flew back to England and stayed at his mate Jim's house in Ipswich. Ritchie knew Jim, now a civilian, when he was a Corporal in the Royal Engineers at Hameln and stayed with him and his wife for the rest of his leave. "They were great company, but the main reason for staying at their house was because I was having sex with one of their very attractive neighbours, I hadn't had sex for so long that I was making up for that lost time out in Iraq."

After his leave had finished Ritchie returned to the Dental Centre at Osnabruck and promptly stuck his thumb up his arse and his mind in neutral, he was going to make a point of doing absolutely nothing for the British Army in general, and even less for the RADC personally. From July to August he went on a Professional Selling Course at the Army Resettlement Centre in Catterick Garrison in Yorkshire, it was the only course available to Ritchie because the Resettlement staff needed at least one years notice to allocate him a place on a particular course. If he hadn't been pissing about and wasting his time in Iraq he would have had a better chance of getting on a decent course. For the duration of the six-week course Ritchie was accommodated in Catterick's Garrison Sergeant's Mess, every night after the course dismissed he continued with his own personal and punishing fitness regime.

After his final medical Ritchie handed in his MOD 90 Identity Card and was finally discharged from the British Army in Aldershot. It was at this time Ritchie thought,

'Fucking hell, what am I going to do with my life'. He wrote to his friend Jim and his wife in Ipswich and asked if he could stay with them for a while and would they mind if he also carried on having sex with their rather attractive neighbour. As with all good friends they readily agreed for Ritchie to move into their spare bedroom; they also didn't mind him using the spare room to carry out his noisy horizontal aerobics with their rather attractive neighbour. After eight months, Ritchie had outstayed his welcome, not that Jim and his wife complained, they seemed to have resigned themselves to the fact that Ritchie was now a permanent fixture in their home. But Ritchie knew it was unfair to impose on them any longer and he rented a grotty little flat in Stowmarket at a cost of £300 a month, Ritchie was clueless about how much he should pay for rent and was clearly getting ripped off, he was also aware that he was paying rent that he couldn't afford.

At this time Ritchie was working for an insurance broker as an insurance salesman, he particularly hated the job because his office manager wanted Ritchie to sell the most expensive policies to people who didn't even need the cover, and this included selling to the old and vulnerable. The last straw that broke Ritchie's back was when his manager remonstrated with him about not selling yet another policy to an old gentleman who had more insurance policies than Lloyds of London. "I couldn't ethically do it" says Ritchie and he left the firm. A mixture of jobs followed, from general labouring to a mind numbing job rewinding and packing videos in a video factory, at one stage he worked as a butchers labourer humping meat around a Cold store, this wasn't the sort of humping that Ritchie liked to do. One weekend Ritchie went to visit an old friend called Stevie Reed, another ex RADC soldier, at the time Stevie was a policeman in the Surrey Constabulary and he advised Ritchie to, "Come and join the police force mate, it's a great laugh." Ritchie was broke, in a shit job, and remembering his epiphany whilst being watch keeper out in Iraq, he realised he couldn't get much lower in the food chain than where he was at that time. Joining the police force could be the answer to all his problems.

In December 1992 Ritchie went to the Police Training Centre at Ashford in Kent and after completing the fifteen-week course he was posted to Portsmouth, he lived the life of Riley in the Police single accommodation in Portsmouth for eighteen months. Too many pints and an excess of curries led to Ritchie piling on the pounds, this was a great life, but he was still in a similar situation to that of his army career, albeit he was doing less exercise. He needed to sort himself out and that is exactly what he did, he moved out of the police accommodation and bought a house in Fareham and went back on his strict regime of exercise at the end of every working day. He lost his extra pounds in weight and when the opportunity came up to go on a course to become a Detective, he jumped at the chance, passed the course, and was posted to Fareham Police Station as a Detective Constable. One side of Ritchie's life hadn't changed though; he was still having sex with as many women as he could muster, with his good looks, natural charm, and wit, it was like shooting fish in a barrel.

In 1996 Ritchie's old mate Bob Darkin was posted to an RAMC unit in Portsmouth and had been promoted to Warrant Officer RQMS, whilst waiting for the army to allocate him and his second wife Tania a Married Quarter, he asked Ritchie if he could put them up in his spare bedroom for a couple of days. They ended up staying for eight weeks. Ritchie hit a bit of a dry spot in his sex life at this time and was as frustrated as the time he spent out in Iraq, adding to his frustration, Bob's wife Tania had started to feminise Ritchie's house, she and Bob also had noisy sex which he could hear through the bedroom walls, even his Black Sabbath records couldn't drown out the sounds. His friend Jim in Ipswich must have been laughing up his sleeve. Things were about to change for Ritchie in his personal life though when he started chatting up a clerk called Lisa who worked in Fareham Police Station; she had a striking resemblance, both facially and physically, to the page three model Samantha Fox. Everyone in the station knew of Ritchie's penchant for beautiful women and he was definitely making a move on Lisa, on a five minute break he sat on the edge of her desk and dazzled her with his wit and charm, after the break he went back to his office to get on with his work, Lisa turned to a female colleague at the next desk and said, "I'm going to marry that man one day."

A couple of years later Ritchie was posted to Aldershot on promotion to Sergeant, whilst out on the beat with another uniformed constable they saw a group of eight year olds jumping off a wall and making a lot of noise. Ritchie, wanting to impress the young constable next to him, shouted, "Oi you lot! Get off that wall, stop making a racket and piss off home." The lads momentarily stopped what they were doing, and as Ritchie and his colleague walked past them, one of the young lads shouted, "Hey copper! If I had talked to you like that, you would have nicked me, but because you're a policeman you think you can treat everyone like shit!" Suitably chastened Ritchie said, "Actually you're quite right, I'm sorry for swearing at you and your friends." The cheeky young lad then said, "Good, now on your way lad!"

Ritchie was posted to Gosport police station in Portsmouth on promotion to Detective Sergeant, and after running into Lisa who was still working at the Fareham nick they started having a relationship that was strictly based on what Ritchie wanted only, he told her, "You can move into my house for one day every week and you can bring your toothbrush, just your toothbrush mind, do not bring anything else with you. If you want, you can temporarily leave the aforementioned toothbrush in my bathroom for the foreseeable future."

Over the years Ritchie has worked all hours of the day, if phoned up in the early hours of the morning because someone had been murdered, he would be one of the first on scene; he constantly strived to be at the top of his game. As a result of his hard work and dedication to police work he was eventually promoted up through the ranks of Inspector to Detective Chief Inspector and he is currently working in London as a Superintendent, his equivalent rank and position in the British Army would be Lieutenant Colonel.

Ritchie still lives in Fareham and not far from his closest of friends, Bob Darkin, he lives with his long suffering wife Lisa and their beautiful daughter Eleanor (a combination of their initials L and R).

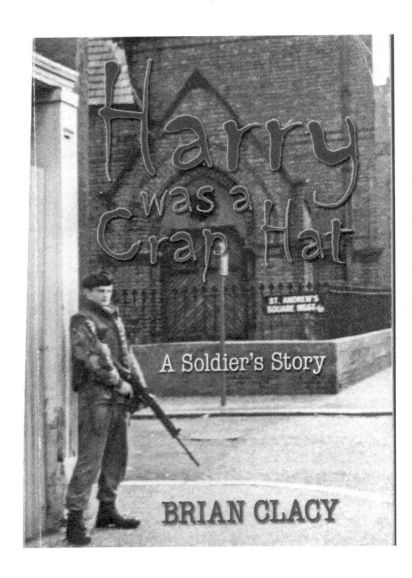

HARRY always WAS A CRAP HAT

Brian (Harry) Clacy

RICKSHAWS, CAMELS AND TAXIS

Rogues, Ruffians and Officers of the
Royal Corps of Transport

Written by **Brian (Harry) Clacy**

Printed in Great Britain
by Amazon